I Love You, Be Well

A Story of Doing God's Will Without Going Viral

Theresa Flynn

ISBN: 979-8-218-72862-5

THIS BOOK IS DEDICATED TO JOE AND EMILY, MY FLYNNS. THIS BOOK IS ALSO DEDICATED TO BEN, THE BOY WHO RUSHED ONTO THE SCENE AND ALLOWED ME TO BE A MOTHER.

"This book is full of nuggets that make you think, enlighten you, and warm your heart. It's the kind of book that you can just bite off in small chunks and grow with...it allows for you to be one with our higher power Jesus Christ. This book is for everyone in recovery and out of recovery seeking insights into a life of miracles. A great read."
Kelly Cunningham, Calm Assurance Life Coaching

"I have had the privilege of walking this journey with Theresa for many years. After turning every page, I realized it wasn't just her story, but also for many others. Although we have shared different paths, we share the same Jesus. Every page reveals healing, restoration, forgiveness, and hope for tomorrow! Each word displays our God who sees all no matter where life takes us. It's a book you will make an excuse to find time to read."
Phyllis Hinson, author/speaker/director of Shiloh Farm Ministry

CONTENTS

ACKNOWLEDGEMENTS

Thank you to family and friends who encouraged me to do my next right things and to put this book together. Robin, Ginger, Steve and Kim's Bethel Church Life Group, The 5/19/91 Club, Coach Approach Ministries, Joe of course, and, especially, Emily, my greatest cheerleader. Thanks to everyone who has taught and trained me to be a lifelong learner and now a lifelong studier of God's Word, especially Dr. Anecia Lee and Phyllis Hinson, for encouraging me to get things rolling for God. Thanks to FreeHeart Ministry for my office space and support. Special thanks to all clients and those I minister to, who bless me as much as I can ever bless them. To 12-Step Recovery programs for changing my life, to those I sponsor, and, finally, to my sponsors in recovery.

INTRODUCTION

This book is a testimony of a person and a project.

It's about a woman who walked in the darkness of bitterness and self-loathing for 35 years but who now walks in the light of love and serves others for the LORD Jesus Christ. It's about a very long journey to fulfill a promise of growth, healing, and change spoken in the Spirit.

This book is also about these short-and-sweet inspirational videos posted on Facebook that were impactful but were not what the world calls successful. None of those videos went viral, and neither did the woman who made them. The videos were made because I felt called by God to do it. Learning to live a transformed life came about for the same reason.

I believe both of these testimonies count, because I believe their stories can encourage others to embrace patience in their journey to change and to understand that we should not dismiss long-suffering. Just as I believe every person is made in God's image and therefore has value, just like the work each of us does for the Kingdom of God is useful even if it's done in secret, so the words of my testimony and the words of my weekly outreach videos can be used for good.

The overall message: sometimes we have to wait.

Also: sometimes we have to just do what God says and know that we may not fully understand it all.

And this: Sometimes we can be proud of our accomplishments, even if they don't make us famous, rich, or have rock-hard abs. Yes, even in today's world of influencers, celebrities, and millionaires.

As soon as I made the decision to leave atheism and addiction to go all-in for Jesus, I believe a goal was assigned to me, and that was to "heal

Christians." Not knowing exactly how that would look, I just took care of myself for many years with a way of life called recovery, and served willingly in every church I attended and in several ministries. I waited and worked until I knew how to do what God wanted from me. Nearly 20 years into the journey, I managed to finish my training and launched a practice to biblically coach and counsel believers of all kinds. I learned to do all the small business things and even made online content to share weekly videos as a form of outreach. Each was around 5 minutes in length, and I hoped each topic would inspire people with the kind of experience, strength, and biblical hope that improved my life and my relationship with God. I always tried to include the scriptures God brought to my mind as I was recording.

The goal was to get a specific two-fold message out:

Fellow Christians, it is time to do the work to heal!

Doubtful ones, come inside where it's warm; God loves you, I promise!

I wanted social media followers to hear some of God's amazing truths and some of the principles that I live by, with the goal of encouraging others to reach that next level of victory for God. I hoped the messages would be re-posted everywhere. They were not. But now, as I share some of my backstory alongside some of those weekly messages, perhaps you will be able to appreciate a few things. The first is that unbelievers can indeed become believers in Jesus. The next is that believers can indeed grow in their faith and stay focused on the living God even when faced with great darkness, difficulty, and death.

There came a time when I decided to stop producing weekly posts. I wasn't concerned that I hadn't gone "viral." I wasn't discouraged that I hadn't received the views that other "influencers" seem to get. I felt called to stop, but God showed me that I did work hard, and I realized I was proud of my work. *I had hundreds of views! I had a few shares!*

I realized I had encouraged myself as I attempted to encourage others. And I (a former anger and impatience addict) had persevered to learn how to do all kinds of technology in order to accomplish my goals; I had done something!

I accept without regret how long it took me to get to the point where I had something to say and do for the Kingdom of God. I came into the Body of Christ in my mid-30s with lifelong issues with body image, an eating disorder, and a negative anti-Christian mindset. Years later, I am someone able and willing to connect to Jesus my LORD and Savior one day at a time, loving others, including myself. God taught me slowly how to be of service to myself and others and to follow Him just a little bit more through each season. It took almost 20 years of growing up in Christ. It took all that time to turn my former life around. I healed, studied, and repaired relationships; I suffered great loss, and I did the next right thing.

What do I hope you will receive from this project? I hope you will get inspired as you join me in the memories. However you found the book, join me in watching a faith unfold. If you believe in God or not, still join me. You are loved, and there is room for you.

From the beginning of 2023 to the beginning of 2025, I ended most of the videos by saying "I love you, be well." Each video was totally unscripted (except one, which ended up being read from a script as a voice-only post). I received a topic from God and did a study on the Scriptures that came to me, but the recordings were one-take and unedited. Much thanks to Facebook and Canva for allowing a novice to create colorful, polished videos that also included relevant scriptures.

This project is organized into chapters with a general theme. I have included edited and refined transcripts from relevant video messages, along with a testimony of how God changed me and now uses me - getting from point A to point here, essentially. May you be encouraged by these TAVI Tuesday topics, and may you connect with the broadbrush testimony that begins each chapter. All Bible scriptures referenced or written are taken from the King James Version. I study from many versions, and while KJV is one of my favorite translations, it is also in the public domain. *This book was written without the use of Artificial Intelligence.*

Thank you for joining me. *I love you, be well.*

CHAPTER 1

WHAT IS LOVE? YOU MEAN, WHO.

20 years in and 20 years out.

I suffered with an eating disorder for 20 years before God brought me out of darkness. As of this writing, I'm in my 20th year of recovery and spiritual growth. Change definitely occurred, and it wasn't my doing.

A little explanation of the old life should help my new life make sense. I had an overall basic lower middle-class childhood with unique but not unusual dysfunction and pain that middle Americans commonly dealt with in the last half of the 20th century. Defining moments and defining relationships were present, good and bad.

When I think of pleasant childhood memories, I often return to my Aunt and Uncle's townhouse in the Bronx. It was the 1970s, and they had this art deco bathroom with black and green tiles, a skylight, and chrome fixtures. I spent time in there, checking out Aunt Rosalie's makeup and Uncle Anthony's hair dryer; I loved the soft light and the smell of Irish Spring soap. This couple went shopping at department stores in Manhattan, visited my family in New Jersey with Italian desserts boxed and bound with string, and always made me feel special when I often didn't feel seen or heard.

There were already many established family factors going on when I was born, including the fact that my parents were married for 19 years, had three teens, and were about to move from the middle of New York City to the middle of a Jersey Shore county. I always felt like an add-on, and I always felt different. I always thought it was my appearance.

Mom was 38 and Dad was 40 when I was born, and my siblings were 17, 16, and 13. My dad's younger sister and only living sibling was Rosalie.

She could not have children, and while Linda, John, and Joann had good memories of their aunt before I was even born, this youngest niece got to spend quality alone time during my summers in the Bronx. Aunt and Uncle took me to exciting places, they made what I wanted to eat, they arranged play dates with children in the neighborhood of brownstones. My parents didn't have time. My mother worked hard as a seamstress and my father worked hard as a carpenter, though he had several career changes over his life. My siblings had launched into adulthood by the time I was 8. At home, I spent a lot of time alone.

Spending time with my relatives made me feel valued. Even their neighbor Jean was the kind of attentive and loving housewife and mother that I don't think exists anymore. In later years they all would call frequently, and I saved a recording of them singing Happy Birthday and saying how beautiful I was. I am grateful for those and for other pleasant relationships.

There were ways that I hurt, also; I have learned that all of us have a way that we hurt based on our childhood. Ultimately, we are all sinners raised by sinners, so literally nobody is perfect. At home, I very much feared my Father, Sal. There is a square black-and-white snapshot from the early '70s; we're in our new house in Jersey and my dad's sitting there sporting a Van Dyke beard, holding and probably fixing something at the kitchen table, I'm three, and I look like I just woke up, wearing a favorite nightgown, my hair is a mess, and I'm holding a doll. I remember that season if not that day, and I remember thinking my father looked like the devil, and I don't know how such a young child would even know who that is. I avoided him as well as I could, but honestly he avoided me too. He was so bright and possibly had ADD, so it was hard for him to pin any one thing down; it was hard for him to spend time with his family as well. He was usually angry and volatile and definitely traumatized when he was young and his father died. When people were visiting he was usually jovial but still expected my mother to wait hand-and-foot on him and everyone else.

I didn't fear my mom but I feared for her; I could see she was very busy and overworked. Louise was treated like Archie treated Edith Bunker but without the laugh track. I could see that she was a stoic person, and for what it is all worth that woman never complained. But I didn't see happiness. I didn't know why, but I got the idea she was so quiet and sullen because I was the last child around and the least attractive. She and her sisters made their own amazing outfits in the 1940s, and she roller skated around the sidewalks of New York even though she was born with one leg shorter than the other. She was a lovely lady who didn't cut her hair until I was ready for elementary school.

I was her baby, but I was big. I was tall and dark. I had very tan southern Italian skin, very dark hair, and from the ages of probably eight on, the little mustache that dark Mediterranean girls can have. I look back now at pictures of classmates and peers and I think, okay I wasn't that hideous, but self-loathing became my baseline. There was something wrong with me, I presumed. Here I was, an aunt since I was three, teaching myself to read, yet always on the lookout for a casual or cutting remark about my hair, skin, or eyes. Always having my worth rated on the spectrum of beauty when I least expected it.

I've learned that the way we feel about our Earthly parents, and especially our father, reflects how we're going to feel about our Heavenly father. I played on the swings in my country yard and sang to God, the songs I heard in Sunday School, and I always wanted to play girly-nerdy games whenever I got the chance to be with nieces, cousins, or neighbors. I went to church with my mother and was eager to learn about God; this didn't keep me from feeling like I should avoid Him in case I made a mistake and had to hear all about it. If God yelled I didn't want to know. After all, that's exactly what Dad did.

My earthly father was critical when he was directing any attention at me. There were many art projects I completed with him in mind, hoping to get his approval. I would nervously bring my work to him and he would pronounce something wrong with it. I never got help with homework or most anything for that matter, yet never heard a compliment. I wasn't allowed to express myself with my dad and didn't want to with my mom for fear of burdening her more. Yes, this all reflected how I felt about my heavenly father without me realizing it. Then I got angry.

I began to see a lot of differences between families when I made a solid group of friends in middle school. I definitely appreciated the overall values of their Moms being able to be in charge of homes without clutter and Dads not yelling on a dime. I also resonated with their discussions of how to do well in school and have plans for our lives. I felt like I belonged at most of their houses more than my own. I got good and angry, though, when I was a freshman in high school. My older siblings were all married and adulting in their various ways, but there was a situation with my brother and a failed business. It was very stressful and, at the same time, my oldest sister dealt with a divorce, two handicapped children, and one healthy one who wanted to get away. I felt more neglected than usual.

I said one afternoon after school, alone and looking through the cupboards, "If they are not going to give me what I want (attention), I am going to eat all their food." And so began my journey of binge eating, bulimia, body obsession and running very fast away from any relationship I had with my Heavenly Father.

School was my life. This was where I got positive attention for my grades and creativity, and it was where I eventually formed my group of friends. It was my identity. I valued it, and it seemed to value me. We couldn't afford the best of everything, but I found ways to get my hair feathered (my sister-in-law cut it for me); wear the right clothes (there were discount places my sisters showed my Mom); and I always manage to have a decent metal lunchbox that would hold my warm bologna sandwich and red apple, as well as the Trapper Keeper of my choice.

In the 70s and 80s students weren't bombarded with the kinds of social and spiritual bunker-busters that are exploding now, but public schools had recently removed any mention of God (before 1962 schools had prayers and pulled curriculum from the Bible along with other classics, believe it or not). So I didn't need to hear that God wasn't real, like today; I just didn't get to hear about Him at all. The idea of presenting science and literature and history through the lens of the Creator was not allowed. They left it out, and so did I.

By the end of high school I stopped going to church and called myself an atheist; I thought I was quite smart about it. I was a good student and good writer who was the first in the family to go to college, which I did by concentrated will and mettle since my family didn't understand or support my goal. I was deliberate, too, in my choice to turn from God. I remember times when I mocked and scoffed those peers who were genuine Christians. I just couldn't understand their positivity. I married a man who didn't go as far in his hatred of Christians but was simply agnostic, and so it wasn't a conversation we had much. If we talked about it, I brought it up. I was the angry atheist, he was the smart and successful practical agnostic.

So what happened? You mean, Who.

The love and power of God presented itself to me just when I needed it most. God was chasing me down even as I was running from him, I can see it in the rearview mirror now. Putting myself in a happy but godless marriage turned into a blessing from God, running from my family and moving 500 miles away to a small town in the South turned into a blessing. Adopting a child after a tragic abortion and giving birth to another child 8 months later: blessing! Bingeing on junk food every day to numb the realities of life. Carrying deep resentments and unforgiveness, and envying what I thought others around me had. It all eventually turned into a blessing, and it all was because I responded to God's patient prompting. I came to realize that my "secret" eating habit of 20 years was affecting my attitude, and it all needed to stop if I wanted to be the best mom and wife I could be. I was at the crossroads where I could run from it all (which I really didn't want to do) or I could do something. I just didn't know what.

That's when God stepped in. When I tell you I was calling out to the ceiling of our brand new dream house that I had to make a change, I tell you I don't know who I was addressing. When I tell you that I read a random book that mentioned support groups for overeaters and that I went to the 2005 internet to search for that phrase, I tell you I was amazed to find a recovery program that literally described me. When I explain how I would go on to accept Christianity after much kicking and screaming and researching world religions, I admit it's because I experienced a literal power higher than myself that was doing just what my support group said would happen but I wanted to "make the right choice" and not appear hypocritical.

What happened: I began to have faith that there is God and that He is good. All the time.

I want this to happen for everyone now!

God: Large and in Charge

Around June we have something called Universal Father's Week, Men's Health and Wellness Day and, of course, that all leads to Father's Day. Let's talk about fathers.

Some of us have had complicated relationships with our fathers. Abandonment. Maybe not even knowing your father. Maybe he was abusive. Maybe you are a father who hasn't done "everything right." But, fathers, you are needed on so many levels. Fathers need to know that if there are issues from the past that need healing, it's ok to speak to your Pastor, your doctor, your wife, your friends or even a counselor about moving forward. Men don't have many spaces to deal with their hurts, but I think it's time to give yourselves permission to heal. You are the head of the household - yes, you are! - and where you are headed is where your family is often headed.

Can we talk about the idea of our heavenly father? I know that's not an idea some people are attracted to. Some people might fully reject a heavenly father, but if we are walking as Christians, if we believe in the Bible, then we understand that He is Our Father. And that he loves us all unconditionally whether we accept him or not.

I love working with children, especially at church. Kids need to know that somebody's in charge. If you work with children or raise them, if you just have a knack for understanding them, you can see that they do need to know who's in charge. Healthy order and discipline eases their anxiety. Sometimes kids act out because they want to know if somebody really is in charge. They might push the envelope to see if there is somebody older and wiser to trust. This happens especially if they are not getting adequate support and discipline at home.

I like to tell children who are old enough to understand that even their parents are also beholden to and responsible to somebody bigger and greater and them. It's our heavenly father. As adults, we can meditate on this fundamental truth. We understand that ignorance of the law does not mean that you're not supposed to follow the law. The law of the universe, as laid out in the Bible, is that there is a heavenly father and we will be accountable to him. He loves us so much he made us in His image and He desires a restored relationship with us. The Bible explains that original sin, the fall, separated us. We were once united. We were supposed to continue in that state and yet we're now apart. We, as restored believers, have the right to be adopted and be called children of God. We are part of his family at salvation, and he wants to be large and in charge over our lives.

Believe in Him and follow Him and He will lead you as you allow Him. In 2 Corinthians 6:18 there is an amazing promise: "And I will be a father unto you, and ye shall be my sons and daughters, saith the LORD Almighty." In John 1:12 we learn that "as many as received him to them gave he power to become the sons of God, even to them that believe on his name." Galatians 4:5 recognizes what Jesus did, "To redeem them that were under the law, that we might receive the adoption of sons."

This is the father's design, it's his love story. He loves his children.

With a higher father, we can learn to forgive and honor our earthly fathers even if they hurt us. Whether or not it's a difficult topic for you because of your relationship with your earthly father, I hope that your relationship with your heavenly father is growing. If not, I hope it's something that you are curious about and interested in.

Spend time cultivating a relationship with this most important parent. The Bible tells us how to behave and tells us all about our heavenly father's character. As you get closer to him may you feel his peace, love, and joy coming from him straight to your heart.
John 1:12-13; 2 Corinthians 6:16-18; Galatian 4:4-5; 2 Peter 3:9; 1 John 3:1

The Great Unknown

I was on vacation last week at Shenandoah National Park, it's a huge park, and I found out when I got there that it has the largest concentration of black bears per square mile of any place on earth. My husband laughed when, in my terror, I thought it was "per square inch." I don't know if I would have agreed to go there if I had known that. We didn't see any bears, but there was certainly evidence of them and strict warnings everywhere. It made me think of the phrase "The Great Unknown," especially that night we walked back to camp in the dark with nothing but a flashlight to protect us against potential encounters with a black bear. The encounter with a scared deer's illuminated eyes was all I needed to know I was in a strange place!

What is your great unknown? There might be something in your life that you are waiting on. You don't know how things will turn out. What can we do while we are waiting to know, if we have anxiety, fear, and confusion? It can be unsettling to not even know where to look.

I practice a principle called One Day at a Time, and I believe it is a good tool when faced with unknowns.

I would love to see others getting to the place where they may be facing a great unknown yet they can still have the peace that surpasses all understanding. Where they can still have God at the center of their life. And they can still take steps with God's power to continue in their healing even while stress surrounds them.

How do we live one day at a time? When we really don't know what tomorrow or next week will bring, we focus on the things that we do know. We focus on today and its goals and problems to solve. Develop tools to use. Grab an anxious thought and bring it into the present. *What do I know/what can I control/how can God sustain me.* It works.

Thankfully, there are things we can know.

We can know that God is real. We can know that the Bible is trustworthy because we have tried it, and it has provided. A biblical foundation helps us understand that the God who created us loves us and has a plan for each of us, that He hears our prayers and communicates through His Word, the Bible. The "Great Knowns!"

These truths can propel our lives even in times of great turmoil or times when we don't know what tomorrow will bring. It may not be politics or sports that keeps you anxious, but for the things going on in your life and your relationships, you probably have some great unknowns to contend with.

I know that if you will seek God, you will find Him. He gives us free will,

11

but we have to let him in and trust Him. He will never push His way in. The Bible says that He stands and knocks on the door of our hearts, but we have to open the door. Once we do that, He comes in and will have supper with us and have fellowship with us. This is something that is not a great unknown, this is something you can experience. I have!

As we go into this week of uncertainty, whether it's what's happening nationally or things that are going on personally, I will pray this week that we all step away from being afraid of the great unknown and step into a position of being supported by the things that we do know. **Philippians 4:7; Revelation 3:20; Psalm 18:30; Psalm 34:14**

Kindness Counts

It's kind of an unkind world out there, but let's meditate on the idea of kindness. Sometimes we have to be kind to others. Sometimes we have to be kind to ourselves.

The Bible says a lot about kindness, and one of my favorite verses is Romans 2:4 because that explains that the kindness of God is what draws people to repentance. That really meant a lot to me as I was opening my eyes and my heart to get closer to God, and understanding that I could trust Him. He's a kind God. He waited a long time for me to accept His free offer for help, after all.

The awesomeness of Christianity is that God's goodness draws us to understand that we are not good - that we need to change things and that we need Him to do it. And His kindness extends to us the very power to change. This is what Jesus did: He came to reconcile us to the Father through His death and resurrection at Calvary. He ascended back to Heaven but left us the Holy Spirit, who convicts us and shows us in kindness that *God is good*. He knows we need to get back to Him, but as a bonus, He makes it possible. That's kindness.

I didn't always think that God is kind, so that scripture really moved me when I first came to believe. I thought He was all about judging, yet it was I who judged others. Now I can be kind to others in ways that were impossible before I knew Jesus. Think about ways that you can be kinder to others; the Bible says that when we're kind to others it benefits ourselves as well.

Be kind. Even if we might need to be kind to ourselves first. Even if there are really difficult people in our lives. Maybe the way that we're the kindest is that we keep our distance from the difficult, so we don't make things worse.

I use Romans 2:4 as a reminder for myself. When someone is hurting me or just annoying me, I can step back and remember that God's kindness drew me to Him. Maybe my kindness (even if it means not reacting or keeping a peaceful distance) can draw someone to Jesus as well. Find a verse that resonates with you when it's time to be kind.
Proverbs 11:17; Luke 6:35-36; Ephesians 4:32; Romans 2:4

Freedom

We just had something called the Freedom Fest in my town and that put liberty on my mind. I greatly appreciate living in America, and getting to experience personal and economic freedoms that other nations don't offer. But what about spiritual freedom?

Jesus says that whoever is set free is free indeed. Have you been set free from your sin and brokenness? Because if so, then you are free indeed! Jesus stated that He came to give us life *and* life more abundantly. Do you have eternal life? If so, then are you experiencing abundant victory in this life? Both are possible. In those New Testament letters, especially written by Paul, we read about a basic blueprint for life as a Christ follower. Some people have this idea that we have to change before our sins can be forgiven. But forgiveness is a free gift from God that changes us. All we have to do is believe it, confess it, and have faith.

When we are saved and our sins are forgiven, we are given this opportunity to live a life that has a "before and after." We can leave a life of being enslaved to our past and our pain and the unforgiveness of people who have hurt us. We can enter into forgiveness and peace that surpasses understanding. Freedom to live a new kind of life.

We are also free from the guilt and shame of the things that we did. Often in response to being hurt first, we devise ways to deal with life that leave us essentially running from God. That's what we call sin.We now know, through faith, when we're following God, that we are in the free and clear to start over. If you haven't begun your walk toward God, I say: seek and you'll find. Ask and you will get the answers from God. He's been waiting for you to allow Him into your life.

When we're still stuck in bad patterns and habits, or even addictions, life itself doesn't seem kind. God seems far away. But the reality is we are still free if we believe. We can get very attached to the ways that we came up to live our lives and forfeit the freedom and joy that comes from honesty with Jesus.

It can feel like just a platitude when we hear that Jesus came to set you free. I know a lot of believers don't functionally experience that, and we feel like it's something that we don't deserve or isn't real anyway. I encourage you not to give up. Freedom doesn't mean doing whatever we want now because our sins are forgiven in eternity. It's actually freedom from the bondage to that sin, to those things that we're doing that are not producing good fruit. They're not producing peace in our life. A lot of times they're just distracting us, a lot of times they cause us to lash out at the very people we love. Most importantly, for some of us, we can be free from caring what others think about us because we have put God in his proper place.

If you need help reaching freedom there are so many resources. Christian counseling, recovery programs, Bible studies. There are so many ministries and programs, but make sure that their foundation is the Word of God. There are good churches, teaching churches: find one. If you're feeling frustrated and in bondage, I encourage you to know that God is waiting to free you.

John 10:10; Romans 6:16-18; Isaiah 53:6; Proverbs 29:2

Making God Look Good

I would like to extend peace to you, the kind of peace that is life-changing and relationship-changing. The kind of peace I firmly believe comes from God. Won't you get to know him now and know him better?

There are so many things in the world that don't promote real peace. Even the things we see and listen to promote distressing feelings that linger in ways we don't even realize. We can get caught up in so many things. We can get caught up in politics, etc. How do we navigate life and the world around us with our integrity intact and our hearts at peace?

When others see us thriving and not freaking out over life's struggles, doesn't that make God look good? We can be in difficult relationships, we can be faced with the consequences of our own choices, we can even be hit with events that are life-changing and completely out of our control. We can frankly just be making our ends meet, trying not to lose hope over the cost of everything right now. And still…have peace.

Even if we have a saving relationship with Jesus we can struggle to maintain a mind and a life that is ruled by peace. Fear, insecurity, and old habits that never fix things can remain even as we begin to walk closer with God. I believe peace can be produced when we can get free from strongholds like unforgiveness and condemnation of self and others.

There are many unexpected blessings from all of that good work handing it over to God. Including the peace that surpasses all human understanding: do you want it?

There are promises in the Word of God that we can indeed rest at night and live our day experiencing peace. Peace is such a better place than fear and chaos and bitterness. Things can be going crazy all around us and yet we can still abide in Christ. We can still allow God to be our master and to allow him to make us rest beside those still waters.

Listen to what God teaches and promises in the Bible. Read it for yourself and read it over yourself as soon as you can.

Depart from evil and do good, seek peace and pursue it. Psalm 34:14

The Lord will give strength to his people, the Lord will bless his people with peace. Psalm 29:11

You will keep him in perfect peace whose mind is stayed on you, God, because he trusts in you. Isaiah 26:3

So how and where do we achieve this? Jesus!

I leave with you my peace. I give unto you, not as the world gives, give I unto you. Let not your heart be troubled, neither let it be afraid. John 14:27

These things I've spoken unto you, that in me you might have peace. In the world ye shall have tribulation: but be of good cheer; I have overcome the world. John 16:33

The peace of God which passes all understanding shall keep your hearts and minds through Christ Jesus. Philippians 4:7

The Word of God is unified. This life is hard and complicated. But with a connection to God through a relationship with Jesus, the One who crossed the bridge, the Light of the world who leaves us the Holy Spirit to guide us now and until the end, we can experience God-level peace.

The New Testament is a guidebook on how to live in peace, be peaceable to others, and be called to peace in the middle of anything. Yes, go to that scenic place in your mind that calms you. I have a picture of a marsh at the beach, it's beautiful and hangs in my office. I look at it often to find peace. Yes, make yourself rest, eat healthy food, cultivate relationships with healthy people, we have got to do all that. But when all is said and done, you are alone. God is the only One who is ever-present, however, so keep your mind focused on him and you will begin to experience true peace.
Psalm 34:14; Psalm 29:11; Isaiah 26:3; John 14:27; John 16:33; Philippians 4:7

Who Doesn't Love a Gift?

Let's talk about gifts and gift givers.

I just had a birthday, and it was double digits (I'll let you guess), but I am grateful to feel young. I feel blessed and gifted by God to have a healthy body considering all I have put it through. The healing that I had from food addiction, alcohol, and other harmful habits really cleared up a lot of physical problems. Forgiveness and peace in the heart also brought unexpected gifts to my body.

This made me think about the awesome gifts I got for my birthday. I had such a good time with family and friends. I wanted to appreciate the gifts and also the time with loved ones. Have you ever heard the phrase that sometimes those of us walking with God can become more interested in the gifts rather than the Gift Giver? What that means is that we think it's great to have another day, it's nice to see that miraculous provision, it's amazing to have those blessings that work out and those doors that open. It's such a gift to get healing for the body, to experience that transformed mind…These are gifts we can receive when we're walking with God.

But we can sometimes get off balance and be more focused on the gifts than the Gift Giver. We can begin to spend less time being thankful for the salvation that God gave us, and we can spend less time talking to him through prayer. We can spend less time getting in the word of God (note to self).

I think about the gifts that our ultimate Gift Giver has bestowed upon us. Life! I live a life with freedoms and in a healthy marriage, and for each of us there are the blessings that we know God has fashioned and orchestrated just for us. Thank Him.

If you're not walking with God, it might be time to recognize and honor that God is the giver and taker of life. Things may not have worked out perfectly in your life, you may have difficulties, you may have things happen that don't make sense, but you still have another day. You still have your health, you still have your ability to reason in your mind, you still have access to the Word of God.

It's ok to acknowledge the gifts but try not to take the Gift Giver for granted. I love Ephesians chapter 4 and also Psalm 68, both reinforce that what Jesus did was our free gift from Heaven. He came down to show us the way, show us His perfect sinless life, to explain to us how we can have eternal life with Him in Heaven when we believe and put our trust in Him. It's a free gift, we can't earn it.

But wait, there's more! He goes one step further and says, hey if you want to walk with me and live with me, I'm going give you something already established from the foundation of the world. Some of you are destined to be a good Pastor or someone's going to be a good healer or a good

17

teacher. These are the spiritual gifts. Free.

What if you heard the doorbell ring. You open the door and there's this gift on the welcome mat. It's something super, something you really love, and there it is. You can do what you want with it. You can enjoy it, but you don't really know who the gift giver was. There's a disconnect. Why did someone gift you? Who did it, what does that person mean to you, should you even trust it?

If you know the Gift Giver, you will recognize the gift. When you seek to know Him more, when you truly embrace a life of getting closer to Him, you'll have more of an appreciation for His gifts because you will know the Gift Giver. And guess what: more gifts will probably arrive. **Ephesians 4:11-12; Psalm 68:18; Romans 6:23; James 1:17**

Fill in the Blanks

There's an exercise I use with people (and myself) that is powerful. It helps remind us how good God is, and the areas of hearts where we can be more like him. An intentional look at the well-known passage from 1 Corinthians Chapter 13 can help individuals and even couples know more about God.

A lot of us may have heard this passage recited at weddings, and it is very beautiful. A wedding is, of course, about love uniting a husband and a wife. It's about God uniting them, as we learn the two shall become one. But we can apply that passage to a great many things, not just a wedding ceremony. We can apply it to someone or something that is influencing us, something we're about to join, and definitely somebody who's a friend or a romantic partner. This is also a good passage to use as a spot check for our own hearts, especially if a closer walk with Jesus and a better outlook on life is the goal.

God is love; are we?

You can read this passage and fill in the blank with the word love. You can also put your name in there, or the organization, or the partner's name. You can step back and assess if the fill-in is representing godly love. For instance, if love is long suffering and kind, can I say that I am?

1 Corinthians 13:4-8 New King James Version

_____suffers long and is kind; _____ does not envy; _____ does not parade itself, is not puffed up; _____ does not behave rudely, does not seek its own, is not provoked, thinks no evil; _____ does not rejoice in iniquity, but rejoices in the truth; _____ bears all things, believes all things, hopes all things, endures all things. _____ never fails.

The end of the longer passage, also well known, is about faith, hope, and love lasting forever and the greatest? Of course, it's love.

Am I easily provoked? Is that boyfriend rejoicing in the truth or is he rejoicing in iniquity? We will fail, others will fail; we can strive to do the God-things but we can never be perfect. But Love: never fails. Sometimes I put in there "my Savior" never fails. No one can be perfect, but if the quiz reveals someone not at all interested in a loving life, what is the next step? This exercise helped me to move forward in spiritual maturity, and I hope that it helps you too. It should never be used as a battering ram against someone, but as a quick thumbnail sketch of your heart and your relationships.

God knows us already. He knows the beginning from the end, He knows what your heart condition is now. He knows where you are in your walk, and what it takes to help you figure out what life is about and to be united back to Him through Jesus Christ. If He is your Lord and Savior, then He is your role model.

For me, when I can say that I am genuinely attempting to be long-suffering and kind in a healthy way, I can see I am representing my LORD and Savior to those around me. When I can take a moment to invite God into my decision-making and pass that other person through the worksheet as well, I can more fully appreciate God's will for me. He will tell me the truth in love, and He has a plan to provide for me.

Are they living up to 1 Corinthians Chapter 13? If not, then we certainly have the right to step aside and look for and wait for God's best and God's love.

Moving Day

Life is all about movement. And moving toward God's target of Love.

The fact that we can point ourselves in the right or wrong direction shows that there is a God who gave us free will and that we need Him.

Sometimes we move locations, or jobs, or move from one season of life into another. Of course getting there is stressful. While it's no fun to play the "no pain, no gain" game, having an attitude of acceptance allows us to admit that growth in our lives involves stretching, reaching, and moving.

Let's bring this to our walk with God. Well, it's there in the last sentence. We are supposed to have a "walk with God;" it's not a "stay still with God." It's not a "sit around and hope things get better with God." It's a *walk*. We need those quiet, still, and intimate moments with God, but the Bible doesn't say sit still and stagnate, it says to grow up and to grow!

I know I can stop my forward movement by taking things into my own hands and trying to rush God, even giving up and wondering if He is there for me. I usually need to just step out in faith (not sit still in faith). The Bible speaks about adding to our faith, so therefore that implies healthy movement and action. We can start with goodness, then add knowledge, we're going to add self-control, we're going to add perseverance, then godliness and mutual affection, and finally love. Despite it seeming like there's a lot of work to be done, when we're walking with God He supplies the energy and He points us toward Christian love as the destination.

It's not about producing people who are constantly trying to do things and constantly trying to perform for God, that's not what forward movement is about. It's about knowing that we have to get through each day with challenges to face, but we can decide in which direction we want to move. Are we going to move through the day with God or are we going to forget about Him or push Him to the side, ignoring His convictions in our heart?

Love for God and proper love for ourselves always leads to greater love for others. Even in stressful times, such as moving or transitioning from loss and crisis and change, we can learn to deal with others well and move forward with God's guidance.

The goal: movement. The end product: love.
Philippians 1:24; 1 Thessalonians 5:16-18; 2 Peter 1:5-8; 2 Corinthians 9:6-10; Deuteronomy 31:6; Psalm 23:4

Eternity

Eternity lasts forever? Sometimes a rough season of life that we are in feels like it will last forever. And sometimes we may hope that the good season we are in actually will last forever. Seasons change, but God does not. He told us about eternity, so we should have faith to believe.

In Ecclesiastes 3, we read that God has written eternity on our hearts. Even though we don't understand everything about God's forever plan, we still yearn for something beyond this life. I believe that is why we find a religion everywhere around the world and throughout history. I think that is why small children ask about God or make comments about Heaven, even if they are not being taught about it at home (there's an amazing story from Joplin, MO: during the catastrophic 2011 EF5 tornado, many children as well as adults reported seeing "butterfly people," most likely angels, who brought many to safety and were seen by little ones taking some people up to the sky). We all seem to know there is something else and somewhere else. Ultimately, we all seem to know that there is a God.

Living our busy and stressful lives now, we can easily sidestep thoughts of eternity. We can get so bogged down we forget that our immaterial self (our soul) is going to last forever and will stand before God as we enter eternity. Even believers can still be overwhelmed, stressed, and distracted. We can all listen to and find influence in the world through our personalized attachments to screens. Also, we can be concerned because there is a lot going on in our lives and around the world. What if we take a moment out of the stress to think about eternity. Where is our heart? What direction is our life pointed in?

In 1 John it says eternal life is the promise that God made to us. Also we learn that, if we choose to not believe in God and to run from Him or fight against Him, eternal life is not our promise. There is eternal punishment. If we, as believers, have loved ones who are still running from God this can bring us stress. Maybe you're reading this now and you are confused, uninterested, or deliberately rebelling against God. I challenge you to look at what's going on in the world. Jesus said before He returns it would be like the days of Lot and the days of Noah, meaning an entirely dysfunctional evil civilization. Old Testament episodes can be studied for themes that show up, as predicted, full-force in our world today. Hearts will turn cold, selfishness will rise, and evil will be on our hearts continually. When Jesus comes back the soul-sickness of Lot and Noah's time will involve the entire world. The whole world will see and the whole world will have to stand before him. Do you think we are there yet?

Confused. Concerned. Curious. Questioning. Doubtful. Confused. Seeking and Finding.

Wherever you are with your eternity thoughts, take some time to think about the peace that can be supplied when we are right with God. Think about your next steps - whether it's getting to God or just getting closer to Him. I have been on every side of the coin when it comes to belief in God and eternity, even the little flat part on the edge of the coin. It helped me to realize He made the coin.

It's a big topic, and it lasts forever doesn't it. I pray that wherever you are positioned right now, that your next steps line up with God's eternal promise for you.

Ecclesiastes 3:11; John 17:3; Matthew 25:46; I John 1:9; Matthew 24:37-38/Genesis 6-9; Luke 17:28-30/Genesis 19

Consider this:

Is Jesus *your* Lord and Savior?

Is God "large and in charge" of your life?

What is your next step in trusting God
to be the powersource for your life?

How can you share what you haven't experienced?

It's never too late: God loves you, and if we
confess our sins He is faithful and just to
forgive (1 John 1:9).

There's so much more with God:
may you seek and find it!

CHAPTER 2
REBEL VERY MUCH WITH A CAUSE

Radical Acceptance.

There are a lot of "nevers" in my story. I never messed up so bad I got suspended or failed a class; I never had a huge blowout with family; I unfortunately never found a way to control my secret binging and weight obsession. I never heard "I'm sorry" from the people I had to forgive as part of my recovery and faith journey, but I was taught to never expect it. There were a few "always" as well: I believed I would always have to figure things out on my own, and if I don't know something I should always keep that quiet; I thought I would always hate my father and other family members for how they treated me and especially my mother. Eventually I discovered that no matter how I tripped myself up with relapses, doubt, and selfishness, I could always keep coming back to what the Father has shown is effective (His Son).

I wouldn't consider myself rebellious growing up. I heard that I was a quiet child, that last chance for a marriage to work and an opportunity to bring some joy into the household. "You never gave Mom a lot of trouble," my sister Joann tells me now. She also, at the same time I was going through prayer ministry for healing, texted me out of the blue to let me know, "You were wanted and loved."

I'm told I laughed uproariously at silliness and at animals as an infant, and one of my first memories is sitting in my high chair spelling out the letters to the word Wesson from the bottle of vegetable oil on the counter behind everyone; my mom used it to fry up the chicken cutlets for dinner. Everyone was amazed and laughed. No brainer: Florence Henderson was spelling this out on tv ads for the popular oil, and I watched a lot of tv. Message: being smart and making people laugh was a benefit.

I always felt a little different. When the family did get together, they talked about New York City, but I had no real memories to share or events to corroborate.

The only time I was mentioned was to repeat the joke that I was found in the alley in a "bad" section of Harlem, a part of the city that was not only outside the section where my Italian family lived but was somehow less-than. The gist was clear. I was not really "one of them." So maybe I should rebel after all, and who would notice?

I did the best of all the siblings in school, and heavily appropriated 1980s New Jersey teen ideals while being raised at the beach. School and school friends were where my identity was formed, and we had a true melting pot of students; nobody really cared about nationality and no one ever, ever asked about religion or church. As I spent more time with my group of pretty middle-class friends, the differences between their homes and mine hit a nerve. Maybe I could strike out on my own and build a life more like theirs?

Going to college became a guiding principle, and I assumed it was a goal I could reach with enough determination. I did. I don't think I suffered from imposter syndrome. I truly knew I belonged where I pushed to get myself. Feelings of social rejection and being misunderstood, yes. But what fueled my resentment was something akin to the Zora Neale Huston quote I read in my Women's Literature course: "Sometimes, I feel discriminated against, but it does not make me angry. It merely astonishes me. How can any deny themselves the pleasure of my company?" Something inside me liked me for who I was, yet my skin color, size, and nose kept getting in the way. I didn't understand it. I didn't see others like they seemed to see me. Check out my post in 24 Hours called "Bullying" for more context.

It took until I was 35 to see there was a connection between my attitude toward God and my inner turmoil and bitterness. Recovery support and accountability partners helped me recognize that I had built a lifestyle of outward success while hating God, and I was catching on that my inability to love and forgive myself and others as God did might be causing my suffering. I grew up hearing that God is loving, and yet there was so much pain everywhere, including in my family and in my heart. So I chose to outwardly disown my Creator and deliberately mocked His followers. Had I finally become the secular hero-rebel that my favorite radio stations, magazines, and books taught was the most logical foundation for life? Everything I read subtly pointed out there is no God, morality is relative, and we should fear the powers that be because they would want to force us to think otherwise. I thought I was countercultural, but couldn't see that I didn't have to search far into the culture to find my godless support. Everything that influenced me was right there, winning Oscars and Emmys and Pulitzers, and either made no mention of God or cleverly mocked Him and His followers. I came to believe that I was rebelling against a "status quo" that was not actually the status quo anymore. In this day and age, biblical morality is the cultural minority Jesus said it always would be. I really had no ideas of my own. I had no idea.

I had no idea my eating disorder and atheism were forms of idolatry. I had no idea that the simplest way to restore my mind and health (avoiding trigger foods and other problems like alcohol) would require the literal Power of Heaven because the world around me was really the status quo and shoves gluttony in our faces non-stop. Wait: to be a rebel was to follow God!?

A miracle happened. The old people in the neighborhood who promoted Bible study - maybe they were onto something. The kind and joy-filled Christians I had met in school - maybe they weren't faking something to make it. The 12 Steps that suggested I look at my own reflection before I condemn others - maybe they will work if I work them. My mindset was changing: my heart was softening to the God who blessed me with my adopted son close to Easter in 1998 and then my biological daughter on Christmas Day of the same year. I lost weight, I lost unforgiveness, and I gained, slowly, one day at a time, stronger relationships and peace that truly surpassed all understanding.

This is the true rebel: to die to self so Christ could live in and through me; to exchange the world's selfish encouragements and overloads for a balanced life and a renewed mind. To radically love my children for who they are, my husband for who is, myself for the broken person I was. To forgive and release those who hurt me and hope for the best for them from afar, and to be filled with love for those who were far from God, so that I could hope to draw them to their own Creator.

May you challenge the authority of this world while under the authority of the One who created it.

Be a Rebel

Rebel, my dear friends!

You might question why a menopausal "good Christian lady" would suggest bucking the system. I hope my explanation will inspire somebody and get people thinking about how they're living their lives and what they are believing in. I believe in my heart that there is a type of person who may feel like a rebel and can do it the right way, by doing it God's way.

I believe there are people who want to rebel against a society they think is oppressive, and I believe that comes from a heart and personality that is idealistic. This is not necessarily a bad thing. These people can see that the world isn't perfect, and even can lash out and rebel against what they think is an imposed status quo. From their viewpoint, this includes any religious hypocrisy experienced in the culture as well as in the church.

These are people who think they are rebelling against a path being forced on them by "the man." A path that restricts their freedom. The sad truth is they are sadly mistaken. Consider that not too long ago, it was rebellious to have sex outside marriage, to display public drunkenness, to engage with let alone discuss pornography, to be disrespectful to teachers and parents, to have children without being married. I am actually old enough to remember the tail end of that era. That was the foundation. What is today's acceptable line of demarcation?

If you're looking to push back, at this point in our dominant culture, the most rebellious thing that you can do right now is to be a Christian. The most countercultural thing you can do in this day and age is to truly follow Jesus, and I say that because if you read what Jesus taught, what the Gospels share, and what the apostles who wrote the rest of the New Testament reveal about truly following Christ...

It is completely countercultural. Then and now.

The world is at enmity with God and always has been. The world system, the way that we've viewed success and review right and wrong, especially now, is at odds with the Bible. True Christianity precepts have always been on the fringes, but the core principles of Western society sat adjacent to them. But now our dominant secular culture has moved so far into anti-Christian principles; I would dare say a true rebel would go full-throttle for Jesus.

Can you imagine? Growing movements of people healing from hopelessness and addiction, marrying and having children, working hard and seeking to solve conflicts peacefully. People who focus more on telling others about God's love than looking for false validation and attention in the mirror and in other people.

You have to admit that the culture does not pressure us into being a Bible-believing Jesus follower. Can we admit we are not being pressured to accept reality, or to be grateful for what we have, and we are definitely not being encouraged to peacefully communicate. We are not being pressured to have integrity in the classroom, workplace, or bedroom. So I say, rebel against it all!

For my rebellious, idealistic spirits out there! Look at James 4:4. 1 John 2:15. Ephesians 2:2. 2 Corinthians 4:4.

You may never have a heart that is stirred to be countercultural, but you may have a heart that's been hurt by people living in hypocrisy as lukewarm Christians. You may have been tempted to find identity and love in all the wrong places. Read up on what Jesus is saying, open your heart to understanding His otherworldly idealism, and find that love, get that justice, receive that healing in God. Learn how to operate out of a truly rebellious higher level than what the world is promoting in this age. **Matthew 23:28; Luke 6:46; 2 Corinthians 4:4; Ephesians 2:2; Titus 1:11; 1 John 2:15**

Tell 'Em Who Sent You

You've probably heard this phrase before: "Tell 'em who sent you." We hear that sometimes when we're talking about going to a fancy place or if we have a discount for something. Let's say you win an award or a vacation. The organizers might say, "when you get there, just tell them who sent you." And when you arrive, the magic words get you access and special treatment. It could happen with a prominent person, maybe in your community or even a celebrity that you really admire. Perhaps they own a restaurant or a resort and they tell you to let the staff know to treat you well. They won't be there but they assure you that when you get there you can announce, "So-and-so sent me," and something will happen. You will have that access and authority that you wouldn't have if you didn't know them.

In terms of being a Christian, the access point is the Word of God. You must have heard this at church, in your Bible reading, or with praying people. You've heard them say: "In the Name of Jesus." They should say it because they mean it.

"In the Name of Jesus" we can have peace, we have joy, we can have healing, we can have restoration, we can renew our minds. And as ambassadors of Christ, as people who are following Jesus and representing Jesus until He returns, we know that *we* don't have the power that Jesus has - we've never really been able to even change ourselves. If we're in a relationship with Jesus we know that He is the one that has done it all. That's the power of His Name in our life and the power that His name can afford us as we minister to others..

In John 1 the Word of God is Jesus. Before our world was created, there was God, and the Word was with God, the Word actually was God, and the Word came to our world as flesh. The Word of God is Jesus! There's an authority as true believers that He gives us by standing behind His Name. We can use His Name and get stuff done!

There's a story in the Bible where people wanted what they saw. They saw mighty disciples and ambassadors of Christ saving souls, in Jesus' Name. They could bring peace and even physical healing, and were standing against evil authorities who were trying to stop the Gospel from spreading. These outsiders saw that there was power to even cast out demons from hurting people, and they tried to appropriate the gift. It didn't go well for them. In fact, the evil spirits that they were trying to have power over by using the Name of Jesus literally beat their butts.

Why? Because even the demons knew that they did not carry the same authority as true believers in Christ. You must know the One who sends you. And He has to know you. Once He knows you, and knows that you trust Him, then He gives you the backing of His Name. He knows He can trust you, too.

Christians should be different from the world. Because of Jesus, we are healing and changing. Confessing sins and being forgiven. At salvation Jesus promised all that, and He also gives you the authority of his name.

He says *go forth, go to the mountain and use My Name to move it. Things will be different, things will move and be powerful because you have the authority of My Name behind you. You know you couldn't see this change before Me and without Me. I'm not here but you can use the authority of My Name and that's all it will take.*

How would it be if I went to the place of that famous person whom I've never met and told the bodyguard that I can come right in. I will hear: "No. You're not on the list."

Are you on the list? If so, tell your problems to the Name who sent you. If you are not on the list, come on in. Get to know and trust God and He will let you use His Name. To appropriate the power and be able to do things you never could do before.

It's a great place to be, to know that I don't have any power but that I can go to my storms and to dark places and prevail, and evil will not prosper because I know who sent me.

Jesus: the Name above all names.
Proverbs 18:10; John 1:1-18; John 14:3; Philippians 2:9-11; Acts 19:11-20

Growing Up

Simple isn't always easy. My simple message is about the difference between being childish and being childlike. Some of you may have been insulted at some point, or maybe your mother as you were getting older would admonish you, that you are being childish. I don't know if any of us have ever been called childish, but it's usually not positive. When we are being accused of being childish (when we are grown) it implies we should know better, we should do better, we should act better. Because a child is going to be very self-centered. A child is going to not understand how to be selfless with the other person in the interaction. A child is not going to be able to think ahead to predict the accurate consequences of their actions. A child is liable to throw a tantrum in order to get what he or she wants at all costs.

No finger pointing here, but some adults can have childish responses. Maturity is a blessing that is achieved in stages, hopefully. The Bible tells us that, when we are children, we do things children do, but then we are supposed to grow up and leave those things in order to move into a season of adulthood. A small child hasn't experienced everything yet. They do not understand how to regulate their emotions, how to weigh the consequences of their words, actions, and decisions, how to serve others even when they don't want to. By the way, as adults we should not expect from children the emotional and spiritual arsenal we adults should have.

However, the word childlike is often taken in a more positive way. When we say someone has a childlike wonder about the world, they appreciate the beauty around us, nature. When you think of a little child and his or her first time seeing leaves fall or fresh snow or a fish jumping out of the water, the first time they pet a puppy - these things are so brilliant and exciting to them. Can we retain that childlike attitude in our life? Can we retain that attitude with God?

In one of those paradoxical teaching moments, Jesus actually says that we shall not enter the kingdom unless we come to Jesus as a child would. I believe He is speaking of that childlike sense of wonder at His world and trust in His uthority over our hearts. We can go into all the theological issues behind that, but to me it means this:

31

Do I have a simple, trusting, faithful relationship with God?
Do I get fresh air and admire the beauty in the world around me?
Do I share love and positivity in relationships that lead to growth, healing, and change?

I would encourage us to try to be a little more childlike this week and a little less childish. Sometimes we can be a little childish, even if it's in our own mind. But in our maturity, we can turn that selfish thought around to a more childlike attitude, trusting and loving and seeing the best in things.

The Bible states that children are a blessing. Being part of a family is obviously the design of nature, but it is also the design of our Heavenly Father. What this speaks to goes against so much of what the world promotes, especially now. Do what you want. Plan your life to the point of eliminating the children that are not part of the plan. Identify as whatever you desire, and if that flies in the face of biological and social reality, so be it. You do have value and worth. You are who you are and should not be compared to anyone else. God has a plan for you and wants you to turn to Him and not anything or anywhere else to get fulfillment and identity. He is serious. Life is hard work but somebody loves you.

Ask God to create in you that pure heart, that childlike heart. Don't try to survive the pressure of life with childishness or think that you know it all. Even when things don't work out well, even when we may have pain from our own childhood, we can learn to lean on God with a childlike wonder, and that kind of relationship with God will last.
Psalm 127:3; Proverbs 17:6; Matthew 18:6; Mark 10:13-16; I Corinthians 13:11-13; Ephesians 6:4; Colossians 3:21

Just a Little Bit More

I don't know if you have heard this bit of American history, but the first billionaire in America and the world was once asked by a reporter: "How much more money do you need?"

John D. Rockefeller's answer: "Just a little bit more."

This phrase speaks to me. Many of us are stuck in "a little bit more." Whether it's a little bit more food ... a little bit more TV... a little bit more screens...a little bit more substances ... a little bit more gossip... a little more time with that unhealthy relationship.

Whatever it is, we're never satisfied deep inside, there's this chasm that needs just a little bit more. So we watch a little bit more, we eat a little bit more, we party just a little bit more. We cheat just a little bit more. I have learned the hard way (who learns the easy way?), and I send you encouragement that there is another way, there is another choice.

We can taste and see that the LORD is good. We can taste and see that God is enough - every time we have that urge to return to sin. Whether it is an addiction or an attitude we need to put down, we can admit that it's not filling the void because we make time for "one more," yet we still need "one more"

The Bible speaks a lot about running to things besides God and how that works out. Not well. It's all about worship. False things are idolatry, valuing something besides God. Eventually I began to understand that in my personal life those habits, disorders, and bitter patterns were really what I was turning to instead of God. I was worshiping them!

If you haven't experienced what it's like to let go and let God, if you haven't experienced what it's like to attack that habit or issue with God's power, I pray that you can taste and see that He is good. You don't have to run to that "just one more" that leaves you empty. God is not only enough, not only scratches that itch and fulfills that need, but in running from Him we are actually preventing God from dealing with our real problem: our heart.

There's a battle going on, and if we let the true warrior take over the fighting we will experience that promised abundant life. Your enemy wants you to waste your time, your energy, and your relationships. Don't let the enemy waste you away, call on God at any moment.

I hope that we never get to Rockefeller's place, where we have more than anyone else in the world but we really think we need "just a little bit more."

Go against the grain and consider this: what if our desire was for just a little bit more prayer, just a little bit more Bible, just a little bit more worship, and just a little bit more healing. God will give you just a little bit more of Himself as you ask Him.

Soon He will be enough; in fact, He will be more than enough.

Moral Persuasion

Faith is a deep and complicated topic, but it's also very simple. It's one of those concepts that you can dwell on for a long time and still need to understand more, but it also can touch you immediately and make life sweet. Hebrews 11:1 says, "faith is the substance of things hoped for and the evidence of things not seen," and I must admit that I have to wrap my mind around this over and over. Simple yet deep. The word faith is used more in the New Testament than the Old to depict our beliefs in God's promises. There are stories in the Old Testament that convey who is and isn't operating out of a healthy trust in the LORD (look at all that God did in the Exodus grumbling of 40 years of willful wandering). When it comes to the New Testament, however, I believe faith is the chosen term because faith enables us to get close to an unseen God who is also a personal Savior.

I speak as someone who did not always have faith in the God of the Bible. I called myself an atheist for years. I can understand that the word faith is special, because the Greek word that was used in the original manuscripts means "persuasion" and "moral conviction," it means "assurance." That means belief. And if you go further into the root of that word in the Greek it means "to rely on by inward certainty" and to "trust." If I can change what I rely on to get through life, if I can change my inward certainty and be persuaded that I was operating from a faulty moral conviction … then so can you. It wasn't overnight, but I could be for you. May you grow as I did to become someone who has unshakeable faith in God. You can become someone who wants to share God's goodness with everyone.

I once put my faith - my trust - in science and the medical establishment, the educational system, politics, even my own mind. I was always using those other (supposedly) moral convictions to come up with these (seemingly) reasonable ways to get through life and to consider the world around me. What happened when I decided to put my faith in God? I was able to recover from an eating disorder and addictive/avoidant patterns that kept me in bondage to unforgiveness and self-condemnation. I was able to look in the mirror instead of pointing fingers at everyone else. I am now more productive, have more happiness, handle my relationships more peacefully, and I'm healthier physically. I know what my purpose is with my time here before eternity.

Where is your faith? What are you morally convicted by? What is persuading you?

Where do you go for help, if you are even looking for it?

Consider where your faith lies, accept that God does love you, and be amazed that He said that with faith the size of a tiny mustard seed God's grace can restore. May you be saved by Grace through your faith in God and may you have a good measure of it.

Psalm 108:4; Psalm 117:2; Ephesians 2:8-9; Hebrews 11:1; Romans 12

CHAPTER 3
TAKING CARE OF BUSINESS/TCB

Ideal Weight.

I learned something important in this journey: I cannot compare my inside with someone else's outside. How someone looks physically or what image he or she is projecting should not define my sense of worth or peace. It's not a matter of sour grapes, insisting that somebody who is thin, rich, and successful simply cannot have a healthy thought life; it's more about realizing that everyone has struggles, and those struggles are internal. I spent a considerable amount of time trying to beat my body into a size that was not natural while simultaneously being bitterly envious of those who appeared able to not obsess about food and weight the way I did. I had to learn to admit that I had no idea what was going on in their heads and that their ultimate value and worth was more than appearing thin, rich, and successful. God wants us to know that life is deeper than the surface, and my whole life I had been trained by the world to keep it there.

I married my prom date the week we graduated from the same college, and we have been a working unit ever since. My husband never said a word about my weight. He's had his own food struggle, so it seemed that we made a wordless pact to keep most junk out of the house. We walked every day in our early marriage (we still do), and would walk a few miles to the local custard stand (a South Jersey ice cream institution in the region where he was training for his career). We would walk back to burn it off our treat. I look at our pictures now and understand why he didn't make comments; I wasn't obese. I wasn't ugly. He loved me. It just took me years to believe it.

In 2005 I came to the end of whatever I was doing with my mind and heart, and consequently with my body, when I cried out in our big new

Southern house with the wraparound porch. When I read a book about emotional eating, the a-ha moment arrived. Yes, I exclaimed inside. This is me! I learned that I am a food addict, and that my life would be restored by God if I would trust Him to give me the power to abstain from my addiction one day at a time. I tried it and it worked, and one key was that God used other people to lead me to Him. The Holy Spirit drew me to Him by using others. His hands and feet.

It's biblical.

I lost weight by eating healthy foods and learning to work on my underlying issues. I had to admit that, just like any addict, I could lie, steal, and avoid reality by numbing out with sugar. Studies suggest that the brains of some people respond the same with sugar as others do for cocaine. Yeah, that's probably my brain. With my mind and body in balance, I could now begin the hard work of peeling back the layers of the past and learning a new way of thinking and acting. The basic principle: change with God's power. The basic realization: it never was about the food or the weight, it was about the self-centered ways I was coping with life until I found a God-centered way. It's a much better way!

I am now able to be of benefit to myself and others. The days start now with God-honoring plans for my food and my decisions, and I have forgiven people from the past and present and practice the humility to apologize for the mistakes I make. All because I started taking care of the business of my life. I became a better mother and wife, what I had longed for deep inside. I have tapped into God's purpose for me. This former unbeliever who was seeking out "all the religions" has discovered the true Higher Power and found the Living God.

One of my life verses is Romans 2:4, and it came to life for me even before I surrendered to Jesus. For weeks my mind kept replaying a very random punk song I had heard on a beach radio station as a teen. "I wanna be a lifeguard; I wanna guard your life." Very well, I thought to myself. Music was always such a big part of my life, random songs would filter through my mind all the time, so this didn't seem unusual. Until the day I was stepping out of the shower and it hit me:

Oh…Jesus is my Lifeguard, and He wants to guard my life!

,

Here I was, at my ideal weight, learning to heal and be a better person while experiencing a Higher Power, and still I was unable to trust Jesus as God's Truth. God's goodness worked for me while I mocked and scoffed Him for years, while I paid Him lip service getting my children christened to please others, and while my body, mind, and life were already being transformed by Him. God's goodness drew me into a healthy relationship with Him. He was there all along, and all I had to do was say I was sorry. His love was and always will be unconditional for me - and for you.

Turns out the weight wasn't standing in the way of a purposeful life of taking good care of myself and others. I was.

Self-care As God Sees It

July is International Self-care Month, and it culminates on 24/7. That's the international way of saying July 24th, see what they did there? The idea is that we should be taking care of ourselves 24/7.

We should concern ourselves with self-care. After all, we are with ourselves 24/7. So why don't we? On the one hand, there are those of us who do so much for other people or for our job that taking adequate care of ourselves is on the back burner. Even as believers, we can feel a negative reaction to the term "self-care" because, of course, we want our lives to be God-driven. We want God to be the center of our life, and the idea of self-care might seem like we are putting the self at the center and not God.

I don't have to tell you that Jesus dropped the mic with His Greatest Commandments discourse. He summarized it all by instructing us to love God with all of your heart and our mind and our soul and strength and to love others as we love ourselves. In all honesty, if we don't treat ourselves well how can we treat others well?

I think it's this beautiful paradox. If you're driving yourself crazy and causing yourself poor health because you're constantly doing for so many others, could it be because you don't have the first phase in the right place? Is God the center of your life and the director of how you take care of others? Because God already said if He is first, then others aren't a problem. Putting Him first enables us to take proper care of ourselves first because we see how God feels about us as well. That He does value us, has a plan and purpose for us, and that He can supply all of the energy, all of the power that we need to take good care of ourselves. And from that we will learn not to pour from the empty cup, but take good care of others from our overflow.

Our motives will be in the right place and our own self-care will be in the right place. We are actually able to live a happy, purposeful life instead of being overwhelmed with the physical effects of neglecting ourselves and lashing out at the very people that we want to take good care of.

Ultimately, it is a hard pill to swallow when considering that putting others' needs above our basic needs may stem from a low view of ourselves that God can't honor, or from a desire to please or fix others that really should be God's job. Take good care of yourself first. God's framework works: God first, ourselves next, and then being able to restfully and peacefully pour into others the way God wants.
Deuteronomy 6:4-8; Mark 12:29-31; Luke 10: 25-28

What's For Lunch?

The phrase "what's for lunch" was on my heart today, and I wasn't even hungry. When we're taking our lunch break it's often a break from our busy day, a break from other responsibilities, and we do think of it as a time of refreshing. But here are some questions:

Do I take that break time to refresh myself with God?

Am I also nourishing my soul and my relationship with God with the Word of God?

Food is important. Even Jesus, when He was in his wilderness season and He had been 40 days without food, was tempted by the enemy to turn stones into bread. Because the enemy knew Jesus had physical hunger and would be in a weakened state. Jesus reminded the devil, and He is letting us know: it's not all about food, it's not all about those physical needs being instantly met. We can't live by bread alone (meaning food and material comfort) but we need to ingest every word out of the mouth of God. That's the Bible, that's our instruction manual, and our nourishment for our immaterial selves.

Let's think about that as we're eating our lunch. Did you invite Jesus to the lunch table? Who's there with you in your car or at your desk? Are you nourishing your spiritual condition as well throughout the day?
Matthew 4:4; Luke 5:16

Inspiration

Often when we start a new year or a new season of life, we have a sense of inspiration, sometimes even a sense of urgency to do things differently, and to do new things. We have goals that we want to achieve. I would remind all of us that we don't have to beat ourselves up, it doesn't have to be perfect, and we don't have to change every single thing about our life … relationships … body … finance goals … everything, in a snap. Expecting radical change instantly probably won't work out well.

But I would encourage us to understand that, especially as believers, especially as people who believe in a God we are trying one day at a time to live for, that we should always be seeking inspiration from God and hoping to be a God-honoring inspiration to others.

We should always try to improve and adjust and shift, so that we are living God's will for us. We can do spot checks all the time. Where are you drawing your inspiration? Is it a reasonable website/person/idea that you're respecting for advice? Are your goals and vows realistic?

It is more than okay to want to do better and be better, but let's remind ourselves that we don't have to be perfect. We have to be well.
Proverbs 3:5-6; Psalm 56:3; Isaiah 40:31; 1 Corinthians 16:3-4

First Responders

First responders are on my heart lately. I extend continued prayers for all the people that were affected by Hurricane Helene and especially the state of North Carolina, where I live. I'm on the eastern side of the state where we often get hurricanes, but to have the western mountains go through this has been devastating. Even before the storm hit I was prayerful about all first responders, in our community and in our land. Often, when I see lights flashing down the road or hear an ambulance in the distance, I think of the willing workers it takes to keep us safe. Sometimes I stop and pray right there for those hurt and those rescuing the hurt in their time of crisis.

When I went through a crisis, I felt I had prayer first responders. When my family was going through intense grief, we really could feel, in a spiritual sense, the support we were getting from people praying for us. It helped us get through our loss and the immediate stress. I can imagine that the people affected by this and other crises, and those who are working so hard to help them, can use our prayers and will feel them too.

In all areas of our nation that are hurting, let's lift them up. Sometimes I try to connect with God, and ask Him who is out there that He would want me to pray for. I will get a sense that somebody can't sleep or somebody is in pain or wracked with anxiety. I know when we connect to God in that way for those prayer points, He will deliver. I believe what we are doing is joining with the saints (believers in Jesus), we're joining with intercessors (prayer warriors), we're joining even with the angels that the Bible says minister to us. These angels are warring and protecting all around us, they are appointed to pray. So are we.

Prayer can be our first response when trouble comes. I thank God for a land of law and order and hard-working men and women that make it happen. When I have safety in my neighborhood and I drive down smooth streets, and the lights are working, I really do thank God for those that make it possible. If I see an ambulance picking up somebody that needs help, I thank God that I live in a community where there is order, where there are hard workers making things go smoothly. Knowing that loved ones and even strangers are lifting them up must feel good.

I think those hard workers really need that special support that our prayers can give. As we pray, the body of Christ can consider what others are going through and consider our first responders who are there to help them. Prayer does work. I know because I've felt it myself.

Philippians 4:6; I Thessalonians 5:16-18; James 5:16; Psalm 34:7; Hebrews 1:13-14

Short and Sweet: Sugar Coated

Have you heard the term "sugar coated?" You know, instead of getting all the gory details or the tough truth up front, people will put a positive spin on the message. Maybe they'll leave a few things out so that it's not as hard to accept the truth. Sometimes we do this when we're setting boundaries, or when we're trying to discipline our children. We don't want to say, "No. You are never going to get that," so we phrase it in a way that is easily digestible.

As I head into 20 years of my journey to wellness, and about 19 years of being a born-again Christian, I wanted to talk about sugar-coating. I came into recovery and eventually Christianity because I needed help with food and sugar addiction. But I am so glad that the people who helped me in recovery, my support system, as well as the ones who led me to Christ, did not sugar-coat things for me.

Those sponsors and fellows didn't sugar-coat the truth; they let me know that if I wanted what they had I should do what they did. Point blank. They spoke from experience and helped me understand the truth about what was really bothering me underneath the eating disorder. Telling me the truth in love helped me to make my decisions and not have to wait around suffering because I wasn't aware of the real problem (me) and the real solution (God).

It hurt at first, but I am grateful I had people in my life who did not tiptoe around. It took a while for me to accept it, but it was what I needed to hear. Question: what are the plain truths in your life that you need to hear from your loved ones, and that you need to hear from God that will bring you to healing?

There are many places in the Bible where it says that to love somebody we tell them the truth. In Ephesians it teaches that we can tell the truth in love. In the Gospel of John, Jesus is praying for all of His believers, then and future, that they should know the truth. Why? If people are telling you something that is the truth and it's said in love, but maybe it's something you don't want to hear, can you step back and appreciate that they care enough to state the facts? Perhaps you are not moving forward because people are beating around the bush. Either way, if they are saying it in love, is it because they do care what is going on in your life?

I appreciate now that I had people who let me know how I could feel better, act better, think better, and ultimately have a better tomorrow. And now I have security, I have hope, I have eternal life, and it all started by me being willing to hear the truth that was said in love without delay.

How can you talk to people more directly so you are not sugar-coating what needs to be said? Yes, there are times when we can approach a topic and massage it so that our communication is done peacefully, and hopefully the person will hear what they need to hear. Just make sure the truth is in there, and so is the love.

Psalm 85:10; John 17:17; Ephesian 4:15; Psalm 34:8

Rest

I hope that you got a good night's rest last night and that you'll get one tonight. Sometimes we talk about the commitment to self-care that can make sleep easier, but sometimes the real issue is spiritual rest, emotional rest.

I do know that I once had a restless spirit, I had a restless heart. Before salvation I wasn't the same person that I am now. I don't want to return! I have actually experienced true inner rest, and I hope and pray that others will experience that if they haven't already. There is encouragement even in a dry season, or when we are in such a state with things going on in our life. Even with the agitation and conflict, there is a way to be at rest and to get rest. That kind of rest is supernatural.

God promises to be with us and to never leave us or forsake us. Jesus said, if you are weary and burdened, walk with me, take my yoke, because

I will give you rest. I have experienced it even through my storms. Psalm 23 is short but it's a powerful way of letting us know that we can go through great difficulty with a sense of spiritual peace.

There's much tension in the air - and there are so many families that are burdened and so many relationships having ups and downs. Frankly, there are so many ways that we end up hurting each other as we are hurting ourselves and vice versa. Push into genuine rest, seek that true inner state that comes from God. It's greatly worth it. I actually have been able to sleep and rest through the storms of my life that I never thought in a million years I could even survive.

I used to be somebody who would have trouble falling asleep. I would ruminate over everything on the struggle to sleep and wake up in a panic, wanting to know how to fix and control and change things and change people. When I put the burdens onto God this allowed me to still be concerned and still want things to work out for the best, but now I can rest physically and mentally. I can experience emotional rest no matter the storm. Seek that and may you find it.
Psalm 23; Matthew 11:28-30

Practice; He's Perfect

The word practice is one I use often, and using it recently made me think about an interview my family did with my church several years ago. It was recorded in the middle of a lot of traumatic things for my family. The topic was "Going Through the Storm" and being able to make it to the other side. One of the questions asked was, what would be your advice to others about going through storms? My answer is what I'll still say today, and that is this:

"Practice."

I had many years of walking out my faith, and that consisted of practicing a surrendered lifestyle. I was practicing the ins and outs of regulating my emotions and discipling my flesh against bad habits. I was learning to take accountability for the things that I had done, to make amends for past mistakes, and learning how to make amends for current mistakes and not being ashamed.

All of that healing that I did day after day, week after week, year after year prepared me for this major storm. I would not recommend the storm that came, or any storm for that matter, but I was fortunately able to make it through with resilience and a sense of healing and hope.

So what does it feel like to practice before the storm?

Times are difficult in many ways; there are many ways that people are struggling and suffering and reacting to stress. I've heard it said that if you are not currently feeling like you are in a storm, that means that you either just finished with one, or another one is on the way. Life is beautiful, but it isn't always easy on this side.

In the meantime, though, we can practice patience, forgiveness, and good stewardship. We've got to practice putting our hearts in a place that keeps us healthy emotionally, spiritually, and physically. There are places to go for help, there are people who we can trust. Learn who the trustworthy people helpers are, and practice all these things so that when it gets really bad, you know what it feels like to do the next right thing. You know what it feels like to take care of yourself. You know what it feels like to extend grace to somebody when they've done something really bad because you've learned how to extend grace at the traffic light. You've practiced not letting every little thing irritate you.

Church should be a good place to practice. The Bible most definitely has the instructions. I am praying for all of us, in the name of Jesus. May we set out to practice living out our faith so that we can get through our coming seasons much stronger, much healthier, and for God's glory above all else.
Philippians 4:9; 2 Chronicles 7:14

Believe Patterns Not Promises

I didn't create this phrase, but I love it: "Don't believe the promises, believe the patterns."

In a nutshell, consider that actions speak louder than words. I didn't make that phrase up either. When we need to assess a relationship, it might be helpful to consider that people can fall into two kinds of general temperament. Now, I did make these terms up: there's the Empty Promiser and the Chronic Apologizer.

I call the Empty Promiser a person who will say that he or she will do something, but only if you do something for them as well. Then, after you have accomplished XYZ for them, they change their mind and move the goal post. Now you are asked to do ABC. You never get to experience the promise fulfilled. Now, I don't want us moms and dads to beat ourselves up because sometimes we have to do a little bit of that to get through the day, especially with our young children. We're talking about adult relationships that should show mutual respect. You can never please the Empty Promiser, and you never receive their side of the bargain.

The other personality is the Chronic Apologizer. I bring up this style to say this in love, because sometimes we can be that person in the relationship. It's not funny and it's not fun, but this can occur if you've got a bad habit, a bad character trait, or even an addiction; if you've got something that's concerning somebody else and you have not made a decision to get help to change. Often there are repeated apologies that produce no change. This could be frustrating, actually, for both of you, but certainly for your loved one. "The best apology is changed behavior," I have heard, and I agree. The Chronic Apologizer may need to get help to change. It will probably not be from you.

If you are in that frustrating relationship with an Empty Promiser or Chronic Apologizer, try to plug into things that keep you healthy:

Pray and intimacy with God
Bible study
Church friends
Kind neighbors and other friends
Counseling, coaching, therapy
Life-affirming influences online

These resources can help you develop a lifestyle of good discernment, so you are not fighting their fire with yours. Acceptance can help you process what's going on with both sides of the street, when you are dealing with the person's patterns rather than their promises coming true. If you're the person that is stuck and keeps saying "I'm so sorry, things will be different," but you just can't change, may it be time for you to make your decision to change with God's help.

With God and those He sends you, you can learn healthy boundaries with others, you can have a healthy identity in yourself. You will learn to value yourself the way that God values you and also you'll be able to forgive and learn how to pray much better for those people that are frustrating you. Note: hurt people hurt people, and when we're frustrated and need healing ourselves, it's hard to step back and detach with love. Detaching means to not try to control and change them, it's keeping yourself safe as you wait to see if they'll do what is necessary. You will be able to pray for the people who are manipulating you as you do the very most important thing: develop a healthy dependence on God.

Sometimes we can become dependent or even codependent in these relationships. You know, you're waiting for that promise to materialize, or you're waiting for that change to happen. You're thinking maybe there's even something that you've done wrong that is causing this relationship issue, or that you need to control and manipulate things to get the person to really have the Integrity to stand by what they promise. The truth is that you should believe the patterns and not the promises. Patterns repeat. Your healthy boundaries and your healthy identity in Christ will allow you to not beat yourself up but also not accept unhealthy treatment. God's healthy promises will prevent you from blaming Him as well. God is not a man that He should lie, and all of his promises are yes and amen. His promises stand.

God promises to:

Wash us clean from our sins
Give us eternal life
Never leave nor forsake us
Give us power through the Holy Spirit to change ourselves and forgive others who haven't

Sometimes the promises of those around us are not going to pan out. Sometimes their patterns are showing us otherwise, but with God, we can stand on His promises.

2 Corinthians 1:20; Numbers 23:19; Deuteronomy 31:8; John 10:28; Hebrews 8:12; John 14:26

Helping Hands

I needed some help recently. The doctor had to help me with steroids to treat a very bad sinus infection. It left my voice shot and my eyes red. I felt bad for so many days that I couldn't even sleep or eat.

I also recently had some helping hands with an office move. I would like to thank the friends with literal helping hands who went out of their way to assist me, including covering both spaces with prayer and blessing. I'd also like to thank the Wayne County Chamber of Commerce for my first office space, and I'm also thankful for the Wayne Professional Women's Network. I attended their first post-COVID meeting the week I started my practice, which gave me confidence that I could figure out how to run a small business in a small town as I watched the inspiration from others.

What strikes me is that, in all instances, I had to open up and ask for help. I had to put myself out there and announce who I am and what I needed. I had to advocate for myself in order to solve a problem. It strikes me that it is ok to need help.

I think a lot of us know that we need some helping hands. I think some of us are desperate for the next step, but we may need to accept that we are the most important factor in whether help arrives or not. We have to ask.

It's very important for us to build resources, to cultivate relationships, and not just to be self-centered. Unhealthy reliance on others is not the goal. It's more about being part of a community, leaning on others and helping them when you can. This way you can say, "hey, when I needed something, you were there for me, so now I am there to help you as well." Helping and being helped gets us out of our comfort zone and closer to success.

This sounds elementary, but I did not figure out all of this until I got my heart, mind, and life right with God. I used to think people wouldn't be there for me, but I had to admit I never actually asked for much help. Somehow, I expected that I should know everything and when I didn't, that people should read my mind. They did not, and disappointment would build. This led to a habit of isolation and self-reliance. Guess how helpful I was to others in that long season? Not very. A lifestyle of not asking for help and also not being there to help others developed.

After my years of purposeful healing and trusting in God, I could be there for others. Because I have been a helping hand to those who needed my time, prayers, or service, now when it is my time to ask, people show up for me too. I know God will provide. It feels good to help others, and it feels good to practice receiving help. Let's not deprive others of their opportunity to be useful just because we refuse to accept help.

One of the quotes that I hear in my church recovery program is that God can move the mountain for you, but he's probably also going to hand you a shovel. He will do it, but He will ask for you to do your part. God is able to do far more exceedingly abundantly than we can ever do but we can't just lay around and wait for it to happen. I have to do my part; you have to do your part. Together we can help each other get some stuff done for the LORD.
Ephesians 3:20; John 5:2-8; Matthew 17:20; Micah 6:8; Ecclesiastes 4:12

Isolation V. Solitude

There is a difference between isolation and solitude.

When we want that time to ourselves, we can assess what is behind it. Personality type and motivation are the big keys, in my humble opinion, to understanding what is driving your alone time. There are times when we feel overwhelmed and want to be alone, and some of this comes down to personality style. We ought to know ourselves so we can be patient with ourselves and hopefully we can learn to appreciate how others tick. Some people are more extroverted, some are more introverted. I have learned that I'm an introvert, so this means that, even though I love being around people, I will eventually need time alone to recharge. This is, for me, restorative solitude. I also know that when I am overwhelmed with life I am also prone to isolate.

Here's the baseline: when you are looking for solitude it will leave you feeling *restored*, the time alone will feel like self-care and a chance to meet personal goals. That's probably also going to be when you have your quiet time with God. In a time of solitude you come away feeling rested, and you're going to feel as if you are regrouping and ready to go back to community fellowship with your loved ones. You will be better equipped to meet your responsibilities.

However, a state of isolation can quickly become negative. Isolation is more about retreating from responsibilities and tensions. It's more about withdrawal rather than regrouping and restoring, and it will always - even when we think that it's helping - produce a *restlessness* of the heart. Isolation comes from a place of avoidance and retreat. It often is not a conscious time to bring God into the equation, and its purpose is not to get back into the world to be of good service. Its ultimate goal is to leave the world behind.

A few scriptures explain the difference between isolation and solitude. Jesus went away from the crowds sometimes, to be alone with the Father and to pray. That's a good habit to follow because we do need to regroup, we do need to take care of our emotional, physical, and spiritual business. It's not about avoiding responsibility and withdrawing from others. It's about gathering strength. And strength from God.

What are you trying to get out of your time alone?

If your alone time still produces that restlessness at heart, I encourage you to be prayerful about your motives. Are you trying to retreat and not deal with things, or are you simply an introvert who needs time away from the crowds to restore and regroup? Group work environments, the Holidays, even seasons like being a stay-at-home-parent, can be overwhelming. Times of solitude can be scheduled in. God can help us understand ourselves and create healthy interaction boundaries while also being respectful of others' styles and temperaments.

Even if you see isolation creeping in, God is ever-present and can help you acquaint yourself with holy solitude.
Psalm 42:11; Proverbs 18:1; Psalm 62:1; Hebrews 10:25; Matthew 6:6 and 14:22-23

Isolation vs. Solitude

Isolation | Solitude

Isolation	Solitude
Retreat/Defeat	Self-Care
Withdrawal	Quiet time with the LORD
Avoidance of:	Rest
(responsibility,	Regrouping
problems, others,	*Restorative*
self-care)	
Restlessness	

Scriptures

Psalm 42:11	Psalm 62:1
Proverbs 18:1	Hebrews 10:25
	Matt 6:6; 14:22-23

CHAPTER 4
REFLECTIONS ON A SOLID THEME

Death Has No Sting.

We sing it in church and hear it on Christian radio, but it comes from the Bible: God can turn what the enemy, and our enemies, mean for evil into something good (Genesis . I have eternal gratitude to God, who saved me out of the blue (my blue) and set me on a path to faith with running shoes on. When all has been said and done, and at this point almost all has been said, done, and experienced by my family, I can review the timeline with peace, hope, and energy.

Sometimes we think that showing up for church is being a Christian. It should be more about a 24/7 relationship with Jesus. At my church, which has been home for over 12 years, our Pastor reminds us that Sunday service is like the locker room pep talk and the rest of the week is the Christianity. The strongest experience that established my relationship with Jesus had to do with forgiving those who had hurt me, and it didn't happen in the pews. Volatile father, distant mother, cruel children, those who hurt the ones I love even worse than what they did to me. It's suggested by my recovery group and commanded by Jesus that forgiveness is the primary way to live a life without the bondage of sin, but I was stumped. I felt that I hadn't deserved any of the poor treatment I experienced. "How could I forgive?" I asked God over and over as I would walk our 86-pound black lab in rain or shine.

God answered to my heart: "Ask *Me* for forgiveness first." What had I done to God, I wondered, that would require forgiveness? I don't go around trying to hurt people like others have hurt me, I thought. Well, it turns out that I had literally broken every one of God's 10 Commandments, including not honoring my parents; a late-term abortion; and the spirit-of-the-law principle given by Jesus that hating someone in your heart is the same as murder. As I continued with Bible study and sought God's direction, I eventually had a brief moment in the Spirit when I felt I was at the Cross where Jesus died, and I caught a mere glimpse of the depths of the sin He died for, including mine. This filled me with repentance for my own sins, allowed me to release those who had hurt me, and produced in me a radical acceptance of the prophetic timeline and the condition of mankind until Jesus returns to restore.

I say all this because this acceptance and forgiveness baseline was where I could operate out of when my young son, a computer whiz almost from birth, was exploited and extorted online and introduced to internet pornography. Watching him struggle with ADHD was bad enough, but knowing his innocence was stolen and dealing with the fallout for this bright but hopelessly impulsive child was hard to bear. I began to pray that my son would sooner rather than later surrender his life and will to the God he came to believe in. While praying and hoping for the best, I began to volunteer for a crisis pregnancy ministry, facing the spirit of murder as women wrestled with the idea of abortion, saving some babies and not saving others, but always unconditionally loving. I stayed hopeful that my atheist husband would be interested in seeking the God he admitted was the One transforming his wife, and I saw him accept Jesus a long 10 years into my own salvation. I was able to be there for my beautiful, creative daughter as she dealt with a brother eight months older than her but nowhere near as mature, shepherding her continuously in the right direction and yet watching her make her own mistakes as I prayed and contended for her in solitude. During this time of intense growth and healing, I experienced an obvious spiritual attack from demonic dark places I couldn't understand at the time but now understand quite well.

And what did I learn to do through it all? Praise in the storm. Speak life and battle with the Sword of the Spirit for the life of my children. Release my husband and wait for him to become his God-version. Eat the food I'm safe with, do the emotional work I'm asked to do, serve others even as my house received my time and ministry too. Listen to sermons and songs; study for a master's in biblical counseling. I saw my son descend to places he would let me know a little about. I spent the most time with my adopted little guy as anyone he knew, and we were close. I wasn't perfect, but I was there for him as he asked for help in his own way. I tried to stay out of God's way as I watched him struggle in his attempts to take the help that was offered, which was everything that would have worked.

It still feels like a dream sometimes, but with God as the hero of the story, I can tell the tale. Ben committed suicide in February 2019 at the age of 20; my mother died of a quick and painful cancer one month later on her 88th birthday; my father-in-law died six months after that. I could take much more space to detail the events and the ways that the enemy purposefully placed all the wrong people at all the wrong times to exact the greatest confusion, sin, and suffering in the midst of my family's pain. But I will take this space to declare that God was there every step of the way. He prepared me by opening my eyes to the battle we are all facing (darkly spiritual) and the power we all need to make it out with eternal life (Holy Spirit). He brought dedicated believers to sharpen my iron and evil people to sharpen my discernment. Through it all and in the intensity of grief, He offered little signs to let us know our loved ones were safe in Heaven.

God uses the memory of bringing Communion to my mother and spending a splendid nine days with her in her widow's townhouse before she died. He uses the memories of my father-in-law stepping up to love my children and raising his hand at our church to accept salvation, which turned into his love for our weekly Bible study. I can recall spending time with the many genuine and decent friends my son was able to have in his quick life, and I can watch them grow up and do well. I can remember clearing out my son's room and finding his gut-wrenching letters to God. I can marvel at how God gave me and my husband the ability to patiently guide our daughter out of her grief and back home where she could be supported and loved back to health.

The Gospel is in practice in my household, even though it looks messy from the outside. The LORD is constantly healing, planning, and executing the most gently radical of miracles one person at a time. Joe keeps making tremendous strides in his ability to be the man God made him. Emily continues to show me what being a survivor looks like. I keep staying sober and abstinent and focused on God.

I have survived, and will continue to survive, the trials and tribulations with sanity and integrity, and it's all because of Jesus. I know what sin is like because I am a sinner. I know I can accept and forgive other sinners, even those who exploited my burdened son and the people who used my daughter in her season of grief. I know what time it is on the prophetic time clock, and I am confident that Jesus is returning. So I keep on ticking.

Take time to appreciate all that God has done for you too. Take time to appreciate the Gospel message. It is Good News for you, and it is Good News for me. Yes, there are mysteries that are so hard to understand, but God taking on a human body that endured a crucifixion and shedding His blood like a spotless sacrificial lamb so that we all can be remade and restored is surely one that holds the world together.

Drop the Rock

It's great to witness the beautiful changes of Spring, the shifting colors, the growth and the green. It's also a signal for Easter time, and I sure wish Resurrection Sunday wasn't just a blip in the culture at large anymore. When I was small I got a new outfit and everything, maybe not the classic Easter Bonnet, but I went to church, I dressed up, and it felt so special. I didn't really believe a bunny brought the basket, but the seasons were changing and I was taught that something special was being celebrated in church.

I was feeling a bit heavy about it, but the LORD brought me images of stones to show me what I could do with it. Maybe it somehow relates to the extraordinary time of the Resurrection. In John 8, there is this powerful story of a woman who was caught red-handed in adultery. The religious leaders (which were the community leaders, period) and the locals had brought her to the public square to stone her, which was the legal precedent at that time. They had somehow spied on her sinful choice, and they all wanted to see what Jesus would do and feel about it. Sure enough, Jesus had something different in mind than the public humiliation they were planning for the sinner and the Saviour. Jesus was the "something different" God had in mind.

God was about to move into the next phase of restoring humanity to Himself and restoring our hearts to healing, through what Jesus would soon do on the Cross. He used His time with His people to teach them simple but difficult lessons on His way to the Cross.

So Jesus stood there alongside a guilty woman, in a lowly position and a scandalous predicament. All of these people were so ready to judge and execute that judgment. But what Jesus did was love. And grace and mercy and things that had not been experienced from following "the law" until Jesus walked among them in the flesh.

He looked at everybody and asked for the person without sin to feel free to throw the first stone. Was there anyone? Jesus knelt in the dirt and wrote with his hand something that caused everyone, one by one, to drop their sinner-stoning rocks and leave. Then Jesus told the woman that if she wanted, her sin would be forgiven, and she could go and sin no more. His intervention resulted in her experiencing not only the grace and mercy to be forgiven for what she had done, but she could walk away with a relationship with the God who changes us. With Jesus. That's the beauty of the Gospel.

There may come a time when we have that stone in our hand and we want to judge other people, or when they have a stone in their hand against us, or even when we want to punish ourselves.

Drop the rock.

We can give it to God. We can meet Him and go and sin no more.

That's the Jesus who died on Good Friday for all our sins and was risen on Easter Sunday for our eternal life. And that's why it is so exciting to celebrate. He accomplished this new way of life for us.
John 3:16; John 8:1-11; Hebrews 9:1-21; Matthew 5:43-48

The Stone Was Rolled Away

I get excited when I think of what was done at the Cross and what it means to me. How is it that in some states or regions they schedule Spring Break so that it doesn't even coincide with Easter? The Holiday is just another weekend and detached from the kind of rest and relaxation that we still associate with Spring Break. I'm glad we still celebrate with a break at Christmas time, but is that because we've made that Holiday all about gift giving; I mean, who doesn't like presents?

Jesus was born and lived among us, but His death, burial, and resurrection was the reason He was even born! It all comes together for humanity and, this time it's eternally personal.

Jesus was buried in a stone cave and there was a giant stone rolled in front of the tomb, which was the custom. Jesus laid down His life as the final, perfect sacrifice to reunite humanity, anyone who would believe in him, back to God the Father. We are born into brokenness, selfishness, and sinfulness because of the fall. We are all born apart from God and have this God-shaped hole that we look to fill. Essentially, that's what sin is.

Jesus died and was taken off the Cross and laid in the tomb of Joseph of Arimathea. He wouldn't stay there! He brought the Old Testament into a New Covenant. This was the start of a new stage and a new age for humanity's history, the age of grace or the church age.

Imagine the people involved with this death scene, who placed this giant rock in front of the hewn-out stone cave. This was a typical graveyard scene, and it usually included that cold and hard-as-stone cover. Nobody fully appreciated what God was going to do, it didn't really make sense until they came back on the third day, and the stone? Rolled away!

Jesus rose from death to life for us! To defeat the power of death for all who believe.

I challenge you to revere Easter week like never before, to have a solid frame of mind as we experience and process what this is all about. Get into the fact that the same power that rose Jesus from the dead resides in all believers. I ask myself as I ask you: can you expect a shift in the celebration this year? Maybe you're here pumping your fists already. Maybe you're not in the Word much or don't pray as much as you used to. Maybe you're not looking for miracles and so you never find them. Maybe you're on the fence about God and find it all confusing. Maybe you haven't heard any of this before.

That heavy stone represents death and that old life that we have before we put our trust in Jesus. At salvation, the stone of our sin nature is

miraculously rolled away (it's so heavy!) and we now have a resurrected life. We have a newness of life that began and will end with God, whether it's through healing, whether it's through a new church or any church. Who rolled the stone away? We might not know, but we know it happened, and the tomb is now empty.
Mark 16:6; Luke 24; John 20; Romans 6:4-5

Built on Solid Rock

Another strong rock/stone image is the foundation built on stone. The Old Testament even refers to the coming Messiah, which of course Christians believe is indeed Jesus, as a Cornerstone. As the strong rock and foundation that would be eternal. This is reflected in the New Testament as well. Jesus taught that if you hear what God's saying and don't do it, it's as if you are building your life on sand, but if you hear and obey, your foundation is as strong as stone.

When the wind and the storm and the flood come - notice it doesn't say if, it says *when* - the foundation is critical. Those who have built their houses on stone will be able to make it through, life will not be so damaged. If the house is built on sand, the wind and the rain and the flood will damage or even destroy whatever was there.

Please understand that I'm not perfect, I'm still building my house and though the foundation has been replaced with stone, there have been storms when I've had to adjust and just hold on. Damage was there already because, as a sinner, my house spent a lot of time on sand. We are allowed to grow in our faith, in fact we should. Strengthen that foundation. Just because you may have crumbled because of a situation in the past doesn't mean it has to break you now.

I hope that my iron sharpens someone else's iron. Be encouraged. Get to your next level. Do the construction or reconstruction work that is necessary. And if you are not in the kingdom of God yet but you see that the world is dark and your life is chaotic, I hope you appreciate that there's another way. If you'll trust what those of us in the body of Christ are saying, and verify it with the Bible, do your own investigation, do your own praying, do your own seeking, you will find a way to build your house on a solid foundation. It's eternal.

Proverbs 16:32; Isaiah 28:16; Matthew 7:24-27; Ephesians 2:19-20; I Timothy 6:19; Jeremiah 29:13

CHAPTER 5
SPOT CHECKS AND COURSE CORRECTIONS

The ABCs of Healing.

"The year that everyone died" is how I process information and dates now. That year, I felt that I would be getting a paid job, which I hadn't had in a long time. As I was raising my family, I wondered how God would put all my ministry pieces together, but I was grateful during my time of loss that I was able to push into the principles of grieving and healing I had studied and was now experiencing. I spent many hours in the spot where my son died. I would listen to the songs God gave me, and I would water the plants we got from his funeral and the many flowers I was keeping alive in the yard. I was tinkering with the guitar, so I eventually made sure to learn the song played at the funeral; I would not let death win and forever trigger me with that popular melody. I watched carefully as my daughter skirted emotional and financial danger, always ready to do the next right but often hard thing for her.

There were many who prayed and some who reached out to check on me. There were also those who were already heavily drifting away, and no harm was done. I agreed to work with an acquaintance at the same preschool my children went to, and I knew this would be good for my healing. No matter what I had studied or what I had learned in my recovery, practice only happens when you do it. So I had to do the work of moving through grief while I worked, like the vast majority of us.

I didn't even mind that I was paid a teacher assistant wage and had to wipe noses and mop floors; in fact, mopping while the children had recess was a time to cry and sing those songs. COVID hit, and I was completely unphased. I had already survived crushing bouts of despair and loss, had already managed to schedule deliberate ways to make it through each day without giving in to the overwhelm. Zoom preschool? Sure, why not. Masks? No problem. Being treated like a second class citizen because...I'm sure you know why: bring it. What did I have to lose, I thought. I know Whose I am.

I saw that this two-fold season had been a spot-check of my operating system, and that the LORD was often in the driver seat. No alcohol, pills, or junk food could trip me up. I knew I needed to face my feelings head-on. I made the best effort I could to stay strong in my recovery as my life and family reeled and healed. My sister had been the primary caregiver to our mother; my husband had been the primary support for his parents; I had always been the strong place for my children; Emily had always been Ben's sister. We all had to carry on, and we all had lost a family role.

In the midst of emotional struggles for my daughter and the season of caretaking for my in-laws as they ended their earthly journey, I cried, prayed, sang, praised God, and managed to sleep through each night. I wrote a short children's guide to emotional and spiritual wellness that I shared with summer campers at Shiloh Farm Ministry, one of my son's favorite places growing up. I eventually transitioned out of the preschool and into the Christian life coaching training that would finally put into practice the purpose God put on my heart nearly 20 years before. Helping Christians.

I have no idea what most people thought of me in our community. With my husband's high-profile job, many know us and heard about our story. I had already survived being a Yankee transplant to a small Southern town and had survived being not-Christian enough for some, then too-Christian for others. I learned early on in my wellness journey that it is none of my business what anyone thinks of me and my loved ones. It is my business to do God's will and to know what He thinks of me. I now have people from my past who know I will pray for them no matter what; I also have had people show up in the middle of tragedy to make things worse but who are long gone because they came up against my Strong Tower, Jesus. I have a new and improved support system that is growing larger daily, and I have been able to pray for others, to minister to many, and to be honest enough to take the down time that my temperament needs to stay balanced and for my spiritual gifts to flourish.

Who would have thought that a card-carrying atheist who thought she knew enough to be a know-it-all would be able to connect with God and survive the suffering of life on this side of eternity? I can count it all gain, and now I can decide to correct course when I realize I have made a mistake. I still do need a re-do now and again, and I still hear from the Holy Spirit that it's going to feel better to make things better.

There is no condemnation in Christ, so there should be no shame in admitting it's time for help and it's time to treat yourself and others better. The LORD is always a prayer away from the kind of turnaround that can amaze the world.

Check On the Lonely

Did you know there's something called "Cheer Up the Lonely Day?" I thought that was pretty compelling, because loneliness shows up everywhere. I read recently that there is a "loneliness epidemic" in our nation. Even with (or especially because of) the internet. I think we can all feel alone even in a crowd, but there are times when a person can feel the *despair* of loneliness.

I wanted to talk about both sides of the coin, because there are those of us who have a heart to minister to the lonely, and there are those who are isolated and alone. Perhaps the elderly widowed, or maybe it's people who have just experienced an empty nest. There are many seasons of life and many transitions that happen when we can feel more lonely than we have in the past. I would like for us to pray about who we can reach out to for an extra touch of communication and support.

Hello,
Those who can feel lonely.

Certainly, there have been times in my life where I have felt like nobody understood, I have felt like there was nobody there to really support me, and certainly in the challenges that I've been through there were times when I felt the despair and the emptiness of grief. Yet the overarching comfort for me is that there is somebody who will never abandon us. There is somebody who created us and knows every part of our being. There is a Savior who is there to save us out of and deliver us out of states of loneliness and despair. If you're somebody who's experiencing loneliness, God is there to meet your need. I promise. This sounds harsh, but ultimately people cannot make that emptiness go away in the way that God can. The pressure shouldn't be on other people in our lives to do, say, or be something that will fill the emptiness inside of us. Isolation is not a good place to be, but neither is never being in solitude with God because you cannot stand to "be alone." Please reach out to others and please make the effort to not isolate on that side of the coin; but please understand that the person or even the place you're going to go, it's not going to ultimately do the trick. It's not going to ultimately be a permanent solution to a sense of loneliness.

Hello,
Those who are used to being there for others, who always go that extra mile.

I would encourage you to spot whether or not you are taking adequate care of yourself first. Discover if your motives are to minister and point someone toward God, the best relationship for the empty-hearted, or if you are subtly becoming the person's god, as they continue to rely on you to meet their needs. Balance, peace, and purpose are the keys.

Jesus is the cure-all for that emptiness and loneliness that you might feel inside. Been there, done that, can't show you the t-shirt because I gave it to someone who I thought needed it.
Psalm 31:24; Psalm 38:15; Hebrews 6:11 and 18-1

Check-Engine Light

Did you ever get in the car and see the check-engine light? It's usually not a good sign when we see it. It's a warning, there might be danger, there is possibly something to deal with in order to prevent an emergency. It's that little sign that nags until we figure out what the problem is and take the time to deal with something.

In terms of my own "check engine light," I just received information about my health, and I consider it a warning. I am going to take steps to deal with my physical wellness. I know that if I make health improvements it will probably spill over to improve the rest of my day, my life, and my relationships. I was able to help a friend out while she's ill, and it's a wonderful thing to have the physical energy and the emotional preparedness to help others. To be able to fit helping others into my schedule because I put self-care into my schedule first.

I didn't take very good care of myself for a long time. I wasn't walking with God, I wasn't interested in healing or recovery, I wasn't a terrible person but inside I was miserable and it took so much energy to get through the day with that attitude. I couldn't wait until I could get alone to sit and stroke my resentments and addictions. It was like I was driving my car without taking it in for maintenance and driving around with the check engine light on, right there in my field of vision. Lurking, yet I chose to deny it was there.

After many physical breakdowns, I now take care of my body, my mind, and my relationships without waiting for another critical crisis to loom on the horizon.

There's biblical support for making sure we avoid the warning light. The Bible says that we should guard our hearts because it's the wellspring of life. When I was in a negative state of living, the wellspring of my life wasn't very healthy at all. Romans 12 talks about renewing our minds, and in 1 Corinthians there are several spots where it reminds us as believers that we are to treat our bodies with respect because we know we belong to our Creator.

If you're a dedicated believer and you've been needing to make changes, here is your permission: don't wait for your check-engine light to come on. Do something to move forward with good self care and, yes, rely on God to push you on. If you are searching, wanting something different but not really committed, consider that the wellspring of your life can receive fine tuning from one who is higher than you. Maybe it's time to seek Him, He is there and you will find Him. He loves you just the way you are, but He doesn't want you to stay on your path, He wants to show you how He does things. Either way, you can get to your Heavenly Mechanic before your check engine-light signals an emergency.

You'll be running better. You'll learn to love yourself as God loves you and be of good service to self and others!
Proverbs 4:23; Romans 12:1-2; I Corinthians 6:13; I Corinthians 12:25; I Thessalonians 4:4

Two-Factor Authentication

I was renewing some office equipment and was asked if I wanted to employ two-factor authentication. I decided to do that, because I wanted to have as much security as I could for my data. I like the term because I can see how it applies to life.

Do we have two-factor authentication for where we are getting our identity and truth?

When I looked up the definition of two-factor authentication, I learned this means "two forms of ID that are needed to access data and access resources," and the whole reason behind it is to help safeguard someone's most vulnerable information and networks. It protects from danger, from predators, from unhealthiness, from calamity.

Questions: are we protecting our data and resources? Who has downloaded the data? Are we only listening to the voices in our head? Are we only listening to the things that we see online or on social media? Are we constantly comparing ourselves to other people?

God has his own data, He has this idea about us and about life. If we get our data from Him we understand that we have value and worth just as He made us. Are we actually safeguarding our most vulnerable information? Are we using two factors to support the points of view we have about ourselves and even about other people?

I will tell you the best two factors to authenticate, and to verify, the system in which to put your trust is the Word of God and to pray without ceasing. Another factor would be the healthy and kind people that God would put in our lives as we follow Him. Sometimes we're not really engaged with God and the Word of God, we might not be in a church, we might not be seeking friends that have godly values. Authenticate this!

How should you feel about yourself, how should you feel about others, and about life and the hope of getting through it?

Where are you getting your data and how can you protect it from corruption?
Psalm 100:3; Psalm 139:14; John 12; 2 Corinthians 5:17; 2 Timothy 2:16

Psalm 19

Can we talk about a really rough time I went through and how God helped? He used the Bible, and it wasn't what I expected.

When I was under significant stress due to a situation with a loved one, it was really hard but thankfully I knew from experience that I could go to the word of God for help. Psalm 19 was not the Scripture that I thought I would connect with for the turmoil I was going through, but when I opened the Bible looking for solace, there it was. Psalm 19. Just the other day I opened the Bible to Psalm 19, and I remembered how special it was to me at that painful time and how my focus on those words helped me wait out that situation. Things are better now, especially in my heart.

Just like many Psalms it has a pattern. That God made the world; that He is good but that there are enemies out to get the author for no reason, so please help LORD; thank you, God, for helping when times were tough; and finally, I love you God. So this Psalm does start out talking about how great God is to create the world, but then it shifts focus onto God's way of communicating with us. There are instructions, commands, and decrees of the LORD. We read what they are all about and there's encouragement for us because we read that if we do connect with those attributes of God through His Word, if we do seek to live by them, by His testimony, His statues, His law, then there's a blessing and a reward for us.

I don't know why, but the way that Psalm 19 ends really ministered to me in that tense time. It says, "May the words of my mouth and the meditation of my heart be pleasing to you, O LORD, my rock and my redeemer." I heard God's reminder to focus on myself and the intentions of my heart during the trial, but to also remember that God is strong and is with me. With that Psalm I felt the strength to endure.

I encourage you to have a relationship with the Word of God. Does it sound silly to have a relationship with a book? The Bible describes itself as a living word, more effective than a double-edged sword at cutting down and dividing. The Bible can get at the soul issues that need healing and the conviction that brings change. It's the help that you need. It's eternal.

It might not be Psalm 19 for you, it might be some other Scripture, but you can absorb it now so that at some point in the future God can call it up. It comforted you then and it comforts you now. You may have needed it in a time of great need, or you may have needed it to exhort you in a time of growth. God does that with His Word. And maybe a year later, like me, you'll check back with that verse and you can say thank you, God, yes, I remember how You helped me.

I have a feeling it's something like the process David went through when he wrote those Psalms.
Psalm 19; Psalm 104; Psalm 7:1; Hebrews 4:12; 2 Timothy 3:16-17

Discipline and Self-Control

Discipline is not an easy word in today's culture. There is a negative connotation that we won't go into here, except to say that what used to be countercultural and underground has now steeped the whole world in darkness. Heaven awaits the moment Jesus returns, that's for sure.

Discipline should not be an icky word. Discipline and self-control are themes n the Bible. Discipline is related to the word "disciple," which means a pupil or student. Jesus' disciples were sitting under Jesus' leadership, they were learning from Him in the way only He could have taught. They experienced quite a lot.

We as Christians should also be sitting under Christ's leadership as we learn from the Holy Spirit and allow God to change us. We get there by reading God's Word, being in a Bible-believing church, and listening to good teachers and influencers about how to apply biblical concepts to our life.

You might be thinking that you could use some discipline or order around something in your heart or in your life. I know I always do. Knowing that I can trust God with the direction He leads me and that I can ask Him for the strength to experience self-control is what keeps me going. I know that He can give me the power to do right. You may be battling physical things that you need discipline around, or maybe it's financial or relationship issues. Maybe it's an addiction.

You want to improve.

You need to strengthen.

You desire to just ditch something entirely but wonder if you can replace it with something better.

If we want to be a disciple of Jesus, we have to let Him be our teacher and leader. He will lead us to greater self-control. With a lifestyle of greater discipline, we can achieve a good measure of the fruit of the Spirit. The last item described in that fruit is self-control. It is not a competition or a checklist to punish ourselves with, but a lifestyle choice to grow those spiritual muscles, practicing operating out of that fruit of the Spirit one moment at a time.

Encourage yourself and each other! Any day we choose to do things better and call on the power of God to achieve it, is a good day no matter the outcome. Success builds on success. Get ready for it.
Galatians 5:16-26; Proverbs 16:32; Proverbs 25:28; 2 Timothy 1:7; Philippians 4:8-9 and 13; Titus 1:8

Teach Me, Patience

Most of us don't "do" patience very well. My own personal definition is, "patience is what I do when I'm actually waiting."

Sometimes we think that patience is something that will be granted to us, a patient spirit or a patient attitude will just come upon us by God, but really our degree of patience can be measured by what we do while we're waiting.

Galatians 5 says patience is part of the fruit of the Spirit, so this lets me know that it's possible only by the Holy Spirit. If I believe God is trying to improve my life so that I'm more and more like my Savior, then I can ask him to teach me patience. It makes me feel better to know that my struggle with patience doesn't make me bad - it makes me human. One thing that the LORD has shown me is that this is one area where we can give ourselves permission to "struggle in silence." The more that we let our impatience direct our words and actions, the more interference it will usually have in our relationships ... and the quality of our day!

How does it make you feel to deal with impatience?

How does it make you feel to know that it is something that God produces in us as we grow in the vine and produce our fruit?

We can learn to live a lifestyle of improvements, of trying to be less self-centered and more God-centered, and really thinking of other people. Often, we will practice patience with the behavior of others. A greater level of patience is one of those things that is going to need practice. If we're looking for a life that is more and more Godly then patience is a great place to start.

Friends, God is so patient with us and has been from the beginning, even as our patience with Him and with others is so hard to accomplish. Good ole people.

They aren't doing what we want, even when those things are heading in the right direction. They aren't changing fast enough; things aren't going according to our plans. We want it NOW.

God still has me here doing the work; I think that proves God is patient with me, so can I be patient with others?

Colossians reminds us that we should actually clothe ourselves with patience. It seems like it's something we need to consciously be aware of and choose to cover ourselves with it. It's not something that is organically just there from birth.

69

How do you feel when you have to wait?

What do you do when you have to wait?

What does patience look like right now for you? Is it a relationship issue, is it something in your finances or in decisions that you have to make? Decisions that other people are making around you? Ask God to teach you patience.

See where it goes from there. Just like any muscle, when we practice these things it gets easier. Patience might not feel good because we usually want the outcome now, but when you can rest in God's promises that all things will work together for the good for those who love Him and are called according to His purpose, waiting can happen in peace.

Galatians 5:22-26; Colossians 3:12-13; Romans 8:25; Psalm 37:7

CHAPTER 6
24 HOURS TO CHANGE THE WORLD

Off the Hook.

I have three beautiful metal hooks I bought at TJ Maxx years ago. They never made it to the wall, but they do serve a purpose. They go with me to ministry events when forgiveness is a topic of the day. For instance, at post-abortion healing retreats, I tuck a blue backpack into the corner of the room where we do the most work that day. The backpack is usually filled with the heaviest books I can find in my home library. Erickson's *Theology* and *Dorland's Illustrated Medical Dictionary* make up the bulk. The pretty hooks are hidden in the front pouch.

We all like to condemn women who have had an abortion and go so far as to actually infer it is the unforgivable sin. I can tell you that everyone I have worked with, and including myself, not only carries self-condemnation, but it often revolves around why they didn't say no to their coercer. The boyfriend, yes, often coerces, but sometimes also parents or church leaders pressure women into these terrible decisions. Sometimes, too, those women blamed themselves for their silence, giving into the fear of reprisal that led them to keep it a secret. When it's time, the women are asked to hold a hook and place the heavy bag on it. We want those who hurt us to be "on the hook" somehow for the pain they caused! Even if we have to carry the hook ourselves, that seems better than to forgive. People have lived a lot of life and hurt in many places with that weight still attached.

What I hope participants experience is the physical representation of feeling the weight and seeing there is another hook, but it's empty until we take the burden off of ourselves and place the burden on the LORD. Even if one person gets it each time, there is an acknowledgment that the burdens on our hook are only holding *us* back and that God can be trusted to deal with those who hurt us. We practice the transfer.

There is a third hook. I use that one to represent the people who hurt us. They get the backpack too. Whether or not they tell us, we have to assume that those who hurt us have their own burdens, and that it may even be from the harm they have caused us. Can we pray for them?

I never set out to forgive people. In fact, I was pretty happy walking around with the discontent of intense levels of unforgiveness and anger in my mind and heart over many situations and relationships. Deliberately forgiving people from the past and meeting Jesus at the Cross with my own sins prepared me for the trials and tribulations that would come as my family grew and my faith did too.

I can't describe what it is like to sleep at night and shower in the morning and not be filled with the what-ifs and the I-told-you-so diatribes that plagued me for years. God has it, the burden is off of me, and frankly, I don't want anyone to perish for eternity, so I am willing to ask God to save them, bless them, and change me. Getting there is not fun, but peace is worth it.

This chapter explores several of the many National and International days of recognition, especially as they apply to wellness. I skipped National Hot Dog Day to go straight to the heart. We can do almost anything for 24 hours. It may take more than 24 hours to change the world, but what if we start with forgiveness and, one day at a time, we release those who hurt us and put them on God's hook?

Mountains

My heart is hurting and my prayers are going out continually to the people in the North Carolina Mountains as well in Tennessee, South Carolina, Georgia, Florida, all areas that were hit by Hurricane Helene, and even recently in Texas. Even though that feels like it was a while ago in our spin cycle of events, there's still a lot of damage and there's still a lot that has been done and is being done. And so my prayers go out to everyone who's got their boots on the ground helping, and for citizens of my great state who are still suffering. I actually love the mountains, and I didn't know that until recently. I always thought I was a beach girl, I grew up at the Jersey Shore, but then I visited places like Boone, Asheville, and Blowing Rock, and I was in awe and I was hooked. I'm actually kind of a mountain Momma.

I like to visit them and to do a little bit of hiking, not the most rigorous but, you know, just to see the beauty out there. And when you get to the top of a vista you can look down and see what your feet have accomplished. You can look out into the atmosphere and see God's Beauty. It's an amazing and beautiful feeling.

I like the archetypal image of the mountain. Immense, immovable, powerful. Did you know we can move mountains with our faith? Jesus said that if we have faith just the size of a mustard seed that we can tell a mountain to move. Think about today, and this week, and your current season of life: what is the mountain that needs to move?

Make no mistake, I'm experiencing things myself. I'm waiting patiently on International Mountain Day, and I'm having faith over stressful issues and remaining griefs, and God reminds me, "I AM working on it!" There are many moving pieces, there are other people with their own free will that the Lord is drawing to Him. The LORD hopes, as I do, that those moving pieces will receive the Holy Spirit and be healed.

Sometimes the mountain is that high beautiful place where we get to the top, and we have reached our goal, and we can look down and see the beautiful work of God. It is at the pinnacle that we can see how high God has brought us. But sometimes the mountain is a stumbling block, something in the way, something that seems huge and permanent. It's then that we must trust God, and we must rest in the knowledge that all things do work together for the good of all who love Him and are called according to His purpose.

Are you loving God today? Are you trusting God to order your steps up the mountain and thanking Him for each step of the goal that is met? Or are you trusting God to enlarge your faith as you wait and watch for the mountain to topple? Let's have faith that He wants what's best and that He can indeed move mountains just as well as He can place us on top of them.

Isaiah 2:2 Isaiah 40:4 Matthew 17:20 Romans 8:28

Bullying

Almost coinciding with "World Mental Health Day" are two National days in one week that are compelling to me. One is "National Face Your Fears Day" and the other is the very next day, "National Stop Bullying Day." I take stock of the awareness days going on each month to see how I can bring that into my God-honoring approach to healing and wellness. I get so much out of bringing the problems of life to God for his safe attention and care.

With these three days appearing so close, I can't help but feel for the vast numbers of us who have experienced mental health challenges. This message will focus on bullying, which is an important emotional and even spiritual wellness topic.

As Christians, we want to make good choices, we want to treat others well. Jesus said we should treat others the way we want to be treated. So what happens when it's a disaster? What happens, especially when we are young, for instance, and have grown up with Christian parents telling us to "just pray" for our enemies? Listen, we are called to turn the other cheek but we are also called to state the truth in love. I believe confusion can arise, because with abuse, turning the other cheek may mean detaching emotionally. This means not enduring abuse and humiliation that God surely didn't plan, and certainly not enduring it at the expense of the Gospel of Christ. It is one thing for a dedicated believer to endure persecution on the behalf of the Name of Jesus, and it is another for anyone to endure personal abuse and humiliation. Stating the truth in love may mean putting up strong boundaries so bullying doesn't continue. The biblical truth, however, is that radical Christian principles can only be applied by radical Christians. All of us suffer when we get personally hurt and we want it to stop. So what do we do when we are being bullied, as children and as adults, even as believers? What do we do when we are faced with trying to get through the day? And what do we do throughout our lives when past pain is triggered or has led to patterns that have affected our lives negatively?

How do we deal and how do we heal?

Frankly, a lot of the people that I have worked with in all the spaces I have been blessed to serve - my own recovery journey, through the ministries I've been a part of, or here at TAVI - have been victims of toxic behavior. They have been victims of, essentially, bullies. I don't often work with the person who is the bully, the troublemaker, as it were.

So what do we do with bullying? How does it affect our mental health and why? For the bully and for the victim, it comes down to the concept of making people big (even if it's ourselves) and making God small. So when you're little and you're hurting and maybe you're being trained to be critical and mean or being told that you are no good, what happens? If one is prone to react outwardly, that pain is taken out on other people. The bully is hurt but is not getting the help needed; the pain therefore is flung at others. Please understand, if you're being bullied or you have been bullied, the person hurting you is also hurting. There's no way that a kind, happy, and self-confident person would act like that.

One thing to keep in mind is that a truly self-confident person usually is a meek person, in that they understand their strengths and weaknesses but they don't need to prove it to the world by making others feel worse so they can look better. That's a healthy person. Try to be friends with those kinds of people.

But what do we do when we are faced with a bullying situation that we are not in control of? I love Proverbs, that's such a good place to go for wisdom and guidance.

Proverbs 17:9 states, "Whoever would foster love would cover an offense but whoever repeats the matter separates friends."

This is how I read that verse: Let's understand that people show us who they are. We do teach people, whether we realize it or not, what we will tolerate and how to treat us. So, if you are in a relationship and you are trying to do the Godly thing, and you are trying to pray, and you're trying to make amends to please God and please this person who is never satisfied and still lashes out, consider this: they are the ones *repeating the matter*. 8138 in Strong's Concordance for repeateth means "to do again" or "to repeat, return, do the second time."

You're trying to overlook an offense with love, you're fostering love to cover the offense, but they are repeating the matter. Could it be they are repeating the offense you are attempting to overlook? Either way, they are telling you repeatedly: *We are not friends. I am not here for you.*

Learn how to distance yourself from such people. Learn how to bring that pain and frustration to God. He can be your friend when you are in a friendless season. He can be and wants to be that source for you when you are feeling lonely and want to feel valued. Oh, how He values you!

Proverbs 22:10 reads, "Drive out the mockers and out goes strife. Quarrels and insults are ended."

Can it get any clearer than that? People that are causing strife in your family, class, or workplace, we can't get away from them necessarily, sometimes they are our boss or we may live with them. So how can we drive out that mocker and scoffer who is stirring up strife?

Drive them out of your mind and heart. They no longer are going to affect your mental health or how you feel about yourself. Bring that pain to God, ask Him for the next right step. Often when we submit to God and ask Him in, He begins to shift things. He just needs our cooperation. He has the whole world in His hand but we need to stop squirming.

Don't take the bait, don't respond in words or body language, but literally be covered with the strength of God. Walk with your head held high, and don't let them offend you. Let that person know that you are done. It's all spiritual anyway. Often that person will go away; unfortunately, they might look for the next target. What can I say, they are not healed. But they don't have to ruin your day and your life.

I have tried in my life not to be a bully; I've been bullied so I know what it feels like, and I know that having a sense of confidence and letting the bully know that you are not interested can work. It's also usually pretty easy to see what the bully's weakness is, so sometimes a little taste of their own medicine is all it takes to break the "spell."

I will share a story from my childhood. It was on the school bus. There were bullies and, yes, they bullied others, but their sights were sometimes on me, a tall, dark introverted girl just sitting there waiting to get home. They would insult my appearance, which is nothing I have control over, and one day I had had enough. It wasn't hard for me to think of some mildly hurtful thing I could say about them. I wasn't walking with God then, but I knew I was done, and, honestly, with one comment about their appearance or their name the two hurtful boys crumbled and went away. We were probably 9 and 11 at this point. They left me alone from then on. Did I enjoy lashing out? Absolutely not. But I chose to fight back, and it stopped.

Drive out the mockers with God's help. And if they keep "repeating the matter," then we can learn what they are teaching us. We can separate - mentally at least, but physically if possible. I grew up before social media. Before any internet. Yes, we had cable TV and microwaves. But I am grieved by how much emotional and spiritual bullying is out there online now. The lack of civility, it's heartbreaking. So many areas of our culture are hurting. A lot of it starts at home but all if it starts in the heart. I am praying for victims but I'm also praying for a movement of supernatural grace and mercy on bullies, that they humble themselves before Jesus and be healed of their individual pain so they can learn to stop hurting others.
Proverbs 17:9; Proverbs 22:10; 2 Timothy 1:7

Forgiveness Day

Did you know we have a "National Forgiveness Day" in the US? What does it mean to forgive? Sometimes people think that forgiving is exonerating the person who hurt you. That it's saying that the hurt didn't really happen. It's pretending like things are okay. Godly forgiveness is different. It is possible, and it is critical. Can you imagine if a whole nation forgave each other and forgave another nation? We would be operating in Heavenly levels of blessings, I believe.

What can we do as individuals? True Godly forgiveness doesn't necessarily mean that your relationship with that person is the same or should ever be the same. Sometimes a person is not going to be safe for your life. But real forgiveness is actually for you. Forgiveness is a transfer of the burden from us onto God because we see how the heavy load is only damaging us the most. It is a choice to let God take over with your offender.

When someone has hurt us, we can harbor bitterness and unforgiveness in such a way that it affects our minds, it affects the way we treat other people, it even affects our physical health. We do know that the unrelieved stress of unforgiveness can actually build up and affect our blood pressure, other health issues, and even mental health and addiction issues as we develop ways to cope with the hurt and the bitterness about it.

When Jesus tells us that we need to forgive our enemies, we think that just doesn't make sense. It's not something that comes naturally. Ponder this: biblical forgiveness means that we are not trying to exact revenge, to exact the justice we think is deserved. We finally understand that the person who's hurt the most by our unforgiveness is actually ourselves. We admit we're walking around with a burden that God will gladly take. He has a way of handling it.

Vengeance is mine, saith the LORD in Deuteronomy 32:35 and Romans 12:19.

Are you a believer? As believers we have the blood of Jesus to cover our sins when we get to Heaven, but all sins of everyone will be taken into account by God. Is it a sin to harbor unforgiveness? Jesus says as much in Matthew 6:15. Why? Because we become our own gods walking around with that burden, that need for vengeance we can't do anything holy about, hurting ourselves and potentially also hurting others.

God gets it. The beautiful part of the Gospel is that He empowers us to forgive and even love our enemies!

He understands that it's not something we want to do. When we're hurt we can be self-centered because we want to hold onto the pain and we want them to hurt just as they've hurt us. Even if we do manage to hurt the other person, that's merely an attempt to solve a problem with another problem. That doesn't bear God's fruit.

On Forgiveness Day, think about who you may need to forgive. Consider what burden for vengeance you can take off of yourself and hand over to God. Think about the one who's actually going to be helped the most, which is you. I would call this self care ! You will not have that burden anymore, you will be able to have a different outlook on life and maybe a different relationship with the person who hurt you, even if it's from afar. I pray you experience the freedom inside and the relief from the

bitterness of unforgiveness.
Psalm 103:10-12; Matthew 6:9-15; Matthew 12: 36-37; Romans 14:10

Prayer

As each National Day of Prayer arrives in May, I would encourage us to be intentional about praying for each other and our whole world. I know that there are a lot of things going on around the world, around our nation, even in our own communities and absolutely in our own lives. That's just what happens in life; whether you're facing loss, whether you're facing turmoil, whether you're facing financial difficulties. Life is not always easy, but Jesus is on the way.

I was thinking about what often happens when we hear somebody say that they're going through something. Sometimes we say, "I'll pray for you," but then we go about our way. I've done this myself many times, and I have to admit I did not pray.

I was also thinking about a common mindset even Christians have and that is this: sometimes when we are going through something hard we say, "Well ... I guess the only thing I have left to do is pray."

I encourage us all to reconsider our relationship with prayer. If we are living for the LORD, perhaps we can do better when it comes to prayer. Would a bolder mindset help our lives, our families and our nation? Because if somebody is reaching out to us and going through something, if we have the impulse to say "I'll pray for you" what would happen if we just stop, drop, and pray in that moment? I have been able to do this, and I can tell you it feels good for us both, and God's presence and power are felt immediately.

This doesn't have to be a 3-hour intercession marathon. Are we afraid we will be late if we stop and pray? Literally stopping and connecting with the flow of God in that moment is a very powerful way to be a good neighbor and a good friend and a good family member.

Also, when we're faced with something difficult and we don't know what the next thing is going to be, why sigh and say "Well, I don't know what else to do, I guess I'll pray ..." This speaks to the fact that we think there's something effective we already did or that there is something else we need to try. Many times that is what's happening: we may have done lots of different things, trying to manipulate outcomes. We may have thought our efforts were essential and now that that's not working, we feel we have no other recourse but to pray. We acted like our own gods. But the LORD is the one who gives, takes, away, blesses, and leads others to Him.

Prayer is talking to God; it's sending up requests and reflecting God's Word back to Him and it rises up to Him. Our prayers are a sweet incense to the LORD! Are we connected like we should be, or are we still out there looking for other sources? Prayer should be the foundation of the Christian's life. What if we do that first? What if we pray first and pray for God's will and blessing on those "other things" we are doing besides actively praying. What if we give up trying to make our plans work out and pray for God's guidance all along. Lots of things might change, including our hearts.

I believe if we prayed first and we prayed through things we probably would end up not only with a different attitude - a more hopeful attitude - but we may realize we don't need to expend so much energy trying to make things happen.

We get impatient with God and with others. I am not immune to the heaviness of impatience. I would like to encourage us all to be more intentional, especially on the National Day of Prayer. If we get that little urge to say, "I'll pray for you," what would it look like to look someone in the eyes and proclaim, "Hey, can I pray for you right now?" Speak life out into the atmosphere, speak out hope that we know that God can do things, He can protect, He can bless.

And if you feel like you've got no other place to go but prayer, well that sounds like a plan! God wants that. He desires our connection, He wants a relationship with us but we have to trust Him. Prayer is just talking to God, letting Him know you trust Him, and declaring His promises to your circumstances. Let's look at those areas where we're doing and changing and controlling and all the things, so that we don't get to a place where we say "What now?" We can think our last resort is prayer, but it should be our first line of defense.

Philippians 4:6; 1 Thessalonians 5:17; Psalms 34:17.

CHAPTER 7
ALL THE DAYS SHOULD BE HOLIDAYS

The Dollhouse.

Most of us have to forgive our parents for something. The LORD's patience and mercy while we are in the process of figuring out His commandment to honor our mothers and fathers is evidence that He is the Perfect Parent. I think it was 1979 or 1980 when I spent an entire Fall salivating over the Sears Christmas Wish Book. I wasn't a child who had great demands, and sensing how money seemed tight, and my mother seemed to be the one doing the worrying, I never asked for much. One Christmas my harried mother took me to the local Jamesway (think Kmart) and bought a bunch of board games from the sales bin. Those were wrapped up for my gifts. So, yeah, Christmas wasn't the big thrill it could be for others.

We were always the first house on our narrow, winding country road. But when the new family built on the wooded lot next door to our mostly tucked away property, I got to see the neighbor girl's canopy bed and poofy pet poodle and...the dollhouse. She never wanted to play with it, or any of her amazing toys. She actually preferred to use the two-car garage door as a backdrop for something we called Variety Show. We would sing and dance like Carol Burnett, the Mandrell Sisters, or I would be Cher and she would be Farrah Fawcett. We sang Muppets movie tunes also.

When I saw that the thick seasonal full-color Sears catalogue offered two dollhouse kits, well, I was transfixed. One was a fancy white two-story and the cheaper one was an unpainted farmhouse. In the interest of character, I asked for and then silently yearned for the unpainted one. You know what? I actually found it wrapped under the tree! With a small box containing the family members.

My father never put it together. I asked. He wandered off. He was a carpenter who built our dining room table, it should have been a manageable task. Months later I huffed at him the first and only time, blurting out that if he loved me he would put it together for me. Strangely, he did not blow up, but nothing came of it. I spent afternoons playing with the poseable Doll House Family (names forgotten), making dwellings with boxes and Barbie leftovers.

When I was blessed with my children, I was determined to make Christmas, hear me out, not about a bunch of presents. There was one big gift, one small, and some books and family games. Even before salvation, I knew deep inside that even though I received the only gift that I ever lusted after, the most important part was the relationship I was supposed to have with my father as he put it together and presented it to me. I forgive him.

I loved being an adoptive mom and a biological mom and, though I often was on my own with those two almost-twins, and stress levels were high, we had a lot of great times together. Humor was a common thread. One running joke for my pre-teen Ben and Emily was revisiting their once-favorite Sesame Street character's Christmas video. "Elmo saves Christmas!" They were able to process that Elmo had not, in fact, saved Christmas, but had actually made everyone suffer the consequences of his selfish decision to decree that Christmas would happen every day. We would laugh and deride Elmo as he "restored" things after not taking accountability for his actions. To this day, I can tell my daughter, "that was an Elmo-Saves-Christmas situation," and she will know exactly what I mean. *Somebody messed things up for everyone but somehow ends up looking like the hero when things are restored to normal.*

Gifts don't matter when it comes down to it, but I did make sure my son had all the junior tool sets his heart could handle, and I did get my daughter a doll house when she was around 4. It came with nearly everything, and her generous Aunt Tami bought her all the extras. She played with it for years, and I played along with her many times.

Holidays have the potential to bring out the best and the worst. Whether you need to learn to relax with all the perfection strategies and just be present, or you need to begin to honor your relationships with more intentional presents, may the gift of God's grace and mercy fill you with Thanksgiving and Praise.

Goin Overboard: Do It!

I had the phrase "going overboard" on my mind as we gear up for Thanksgiving. I hope to make it through the weekend in one piece! I believe there are two ways to handle ourselves this Holiday weekend. Going overboard and going overboard. Let me explain.

Don't go overboard this Thanksgiving. We could have issues with food or alcohol, or we could be prone to "going there" with gossip, politics, even religious tradition. When you're with family that you haven't seen in a long time there's a tendency to go overboard with celebrating, but with everyone's value systems and unhealed issues colliding. Let's be encouraged not to go overboard but to find balance. Self control is such a beautiful place to spend Thanksgiving. I know when I can achieve it in certain areas of my life, it feels like victory.

Proverbs and other places instruct us about self control and not going overboard. We are encouraged to have control over our tongue, to have control over our thoughts and to have control over our flesh. When we don't have that it's like we are defenseless. My commitment this year: Even though Thanksgiving is one of my favorite Holidays and of course my viewpoints on certain topics might not mesh with my family, wouldn't it be great if I kept my food intake reasonable and kept my opinions to myself in order to keep the peace in my heart and in the room?

The great news is that God gives the balance you need, the stability. He can provide the control that you might be lacking.

Consider that self control is ultimately a gift of God-control, and you won't risk going overboard.

Go ahead and go overboard this Thanksgiving. Matthew's Gospel describes the scenario of Jesus on the boat with His disciples. The story shows that, when Peter saw Jesus walking on the water, he was so excited that he jumped out of the boat to get to Jesus. He went overboard just to get to his Savior.

Peter went above and beyond in faith, as his eyes focused on Jesus. His trust in Jesus, Who was miraculously walking on the water, allowed Peter to stay afloat. But when he took his eyes off of Jesus, Peter began to sink. This describes the spiritual consequences of taking our eyes off God. Peter started doubting, started sinking, and regretted going overboard in his love for God.

You can approach your Holiday with an overboard attitude. Go overboard as you run to Jesus. Get out of the boat as you settle in to celebrate Thanksgiving and make this Holiday what God would want. Tell others what God means to you, show peace and love that surpasses understanding, and be a light in the darkness if necessary. I hope you find yourself balanced on the waves of it all, with your hand in His.

You just might find it's the best Thanksgiving yet.
Matthew 14:22-33; Romans 13:14

Thanksgiving and Praise

Here at Thanksgiving, I wanted to share one of my favorite Psalms and one of my favorite scriptures. It's short, so I'm just going to share it all. This is Psalm 100 (KJV).

Make a joyful noise unto the LORD, all ye lands.
Serve the LORD with gladness: come before his presence with singing.
Know ye that the LORD, he is God: it is he that hath made us, and not we ourselves;
we are his people, and the sheep of his pasture.
Enter into his gates with thanksgiving, and into his courts with praise: be thankful
unto him and bless his name.
For the LORD is good; his mercy is everlasting; and his truth endureth to all
generations.

I heard a sermon, kind of a fiery sermon on the radio years ago as I was getting to know the Lord and getting to understand the Bible. I was listening to some old school stations back then, but I was beginning to connect all the pieces. This radio pastor spoke on how Psalm 100:4 is an instruction manual on how to get closer to God. It tells us how we enter His gates with thanksgiving but we enter into his courts with praise.

That makes me think. When we say "thank you" to anybody for doing something nice for us - that's very polite, it's very honorable, it's a decent thing to do. And when we say thank you to God, maybe because we have asked him for something and we've received it, we feel it's polite to thank Him. Also, at times when we are sinking into despair we can use this tool to stay centered: we cultivate an attitude of gratitude, so we thank God for every good thing that comes from Him. The food in our belly, the bed that we sleep on, all these things, we say thank you for. We absolutely should do this routinely. That's how we get into the gates.

But there's another level of intimacy. There's a phrase, "singing his praises," that we use when we know someone and we want others to know that person is amazing. "Oh yeah, I know that guy, he's awesome, I get him." Singing his praises.

It's the same with God. We have to know Him, and then we can move beyond just saying thank you; we can sing His praises. We know him because we have a relationship with him. Simple. We're not just asking Him for things and saying, hey thanks for everything. We actually are connected to Him, we are asking Him to lead the steps of our lives, and we're giving Him our hearts, our feelings, our pain, everything goes right to Him. We learn to trust Him. And that's how we can praise God, because we have a relationship with Him. Yes, He meets all our needs and we have experienced it, but we also respect Him for his holy attributes and His comfort and peace towards us. We want others to experience it, so we praise Him in our hearts and we praise Him out loud. And He allows us in, all the more closer to Him. We're in the Courts!

As we enter into Thanksgiving and the Holiday season, we can breathe in God and breathe out the world. Give thanks - Thanksgiving Day was established as a national time to give thanks to God the Creator in 1863. I hope that you know Jesus, so you thank Him on Thanksgiving Day and can even sing His praises.

God With Us

I would like to spend time with one of my favorite Christmas verses from the Old Testament that's also brought into the New Testament story of Jesus' birth. The phrase "God is with us" is from Isaiah 7:14 and Matthew 1:23. *Emmanuel i*s how you say it in Hebrew. The Bible is referencing the coming Messiah, the coming Christ, the coming Savior who would be with us and not far off. Matthew explained that the infant Jesus who came into the world is that very one, Emmanuel.

Jesus was with us, and He is still with us. He walked an earthly life and showed us the way. Whether this is a blessed assurance or the first time you've contemplated it, make the coming Christmas season a time to know God more. He's with us; are we with him? I've seen the memes and I don't want to steal, but it's been said that "many humans seek to become gods, but only one God sought to become human." He did this to feel what we feel, to be tempted but not have to sin, to perfectly model God's blueprint for positive, peaceful living. And all He had to do was live. And grow, and teach, love the lowly and do unconventional things that got Him despised. All He had to do was suffer, die on the Cross for our sins, and rise from the dead. All so He could be with us then and be with us now, as we connect to the Holy Spirit and the power of the Word.

You've had challenges this past year and challenges ahead, no doubt. I promise you that it will be easier to get through it all by holding the hand of Emmanuel because you recognize that He's been there with you all along.
Isaiah 7:14; Micah 5:2; Matthew 1:22-23; John 7:42

Merry Christmas

The Holidays do something to us. Some of it's positive and some negative. I pray that you have been able to enjoy the real reason for the season and have found a place to store your burdens so you can participate in it all. That you can take time out to take time out.

I would like to ask, though, is it time? Time to find a good church near you or time to start studying the Bible. Time to take steps to finally reach God. Is it time to set and reach some healthy goals for God?

I came into the Body of Christ as an atheist, you'll read some of this in my included testimony, so believe me, I know people can change. God is in the business of the best kind of transformation, and that is really what it's all about. Changing the heart posture. Changing our will, our self centeredness for God-centeredness. From darkness to light; from death to life. It's a great exchange!

It's time for Christmas; maybe it's time for change.
Luke 2:11; Ezekiel 36:26-27

Christmas Carols

Here is a little challenge I call "Come Let Us Adore Him."

What I would like us to do, and I've been doing it some myself, can help us stay in good spirits during this most stressful season which should really not be so. The challenge: when you hear a Christmas carol, try to insert yourself into what was going on when that person wrote the song. Most of these carols were written several hundred years ago or at least many decades ago.

We can get really bored with the classics, and we hear all different versions, we sing them in church and our favorite performers record their own versions. And it's all good. Nostalgia can be used to set the stage and the mood. But if you take just a moment this week, when the song begins on the radio, the playlist, or it even goes through your internal loop, listen intently. Listen with purpose, intentionality, and understanding that even though Jesus was not born on December 25th (there's evidence that He was born at a different time of year, probably the spring), we can take this time to appreciate, recognize, honor, and be amazed at the facts that can change our lives!

O come, let us adore Him who was born just to serve us and save us. Emmanuel came to earth, was born of a virgin as a supernatural miracle in order to be a sinless human. But Jesus also was divine. This is what it means when we talk about the birth of Jesus, and that's what Christmas is about. Yes, there are those secular songs, and they're fun, and I like them, but hopefully you're going to hear a Christmas Carol at some point.

Make it not a matter of "I'm just going through the motions." Try to stop and appreciate the words. We like our praise and worship songs now, and even the classic Hymns can still hit our hearts, but those Christmas carols shouldn't be over done, overplayed, and overworked. They should be as special as our other worship songs.

Challenge accepted? I know you will be hearing a Christmas Carol any minute now.
Psalm 95:1-2; Colossians 3:16

It's a New Year

This is New Year's Eve, and I do pray over our communities and around the world that people stay safe. It's always heartbreaking to hear of tragic things happening everywhere, so people just stay put and stay wise. I am so thankful for my recovery lifestyle, so my suggestion is to stay sober as well.

I'm not going to tell you what year I was born in but it certainly did have a 19 in front of it. I never thought that I would see the year 2000, but here we turning into 2025. I hope that people have been able to enjoy the season of Christmas for all the right reasons. And I hope that there's been some good healthy communication and heartfelt goals met during the past year, with relationships strengthening and even new friendships forming. I hope that people have been able to go to church and maybe bring their family members. I encourage us to just keep praying for everyone that we know and love to have a saving relationship with God. It's the most important relationship!

Sometimes I think it's weird that our "new year" begins in the dead of winter. I guess in my mind, new means good and winter means, well, not that good. Paradoxes abound in the Word of God, and I think I see one here too. I appreciate what Jesus told us in John 12:24. Here Jesus is anticipating His sacrificial death even as people were harassing Him. It was not a good season for His humanity to go through. Here is the Light of the world saying, "except a corn of wheat fall into the ground and die, it abideth alone: but if it die, it bringeth forth much fruit." Nobody had seen a person die and rise again from the dead, so no matter how He phrased it, the message was not received that in God's Kingdom, death leads to life and putting to death our selfishness leads to eternal life. But if I consider winter to be the time of dormancy, the time when the seed, so to speak, is in the ground waiting for the warmth and rain and sunshine, then I have a better chance of being able to grin and bear it until the spring.

Rest up and stay grounded in God. He is good soil in which to grow your new year.
Ephesians 4:22-24; Philippians 4:6

CHAPTER 8
NERDING OUT FOR THE LORD

Hit the Ground Crawling.

I can appreciate now the way God made me. A little different. I found someone just a bit different and just a little nerdy like me, and we have been together since 1987. We have survived many things: his medical school training, our grueling decision to abort our first child who would certainly have suffered with a tremendous genetic defect, adopting a newborn (Ben!) and finding out we were already pregnant with another future newborn (Emily!), moving to another region of the country (North Carolina!) that was very different from where we were raised (New Jersey!), financial betrayals, a grandmother who was unable to love our children (or anyone's). I survived the stress of being the breadwinner with a copy editor's salary for a season, retiring to parent with no help most days, weeks, and months. I made it through the decision to get help with my compulsive food problems, which led to a relationship with Jesus, and I endured watching my husband fight against God and therefore me. I endured double-level spinal surgery, friends coming, going and maybe not really being a friend to begin with. I persevered through long seasons of struggle with our son, which naturally affected our daughter, and watched the self-destruction that led, ultimately, to his death.

But through it all my husband and I had our affection for each other. We had our sense of humor and our love of learning and for silly word play. I guess you could say this is how two nerdy swans stay together for life. The movie quotes and the memorized song lyrics have changed from dark to light, but the daily walks remain, as well as the ability for one of us to be in a bad mood while the other sits and listens.

Somehow this family of nerds has found a path of resilience in hardship and sorrow. Wherever we are, the three of us now play Wordle (and Christian Wordle) together every night.

Somehow this family found God.

As I was writing this section, I attended my weekly Christian recovery phone meeting. A phrase that was shared went straight to my funny bone and my silly heart that Jesus loves so dearly. Acronyms are not only so clever to me but so instructive and even healing. You'll find a few in this chapter. The new one I learned at my meeting is WAIT. *"Why Am I Talking?"*

The recovery and wellness journey that I am on has transformed my life and has improved my relationships. That's God! And I know there is still more work to do. He will do it! Now I can address myself, when I have that need to react, to pontificate, to criticize - and ask myself WAIT… *Why Am I Talking?* If it's to know it all, if it's to make a case that Jesus can easily defend for Himself, if it's to bemoan something I'm losing hope over, then perhaps I can remember this acronym and stay quiet. Until further notice. This is another clever little tool in my growth, healing, and change toolbox. Feel free to use it in your own journey to God's better life for you!

I hope you will enjoy these interesting and edifying tidbits and will catch the excitement over the words we use and why they do matter in our lives and in our culture. Reflection has shown me that what most of what we think is up to us really is not. Even many of the words we say are from the Bible, and therefore the foundation is indeed God whether we acknowledge it or not.

FEAR Changes Things

We've got a few nerdy things to sink our teeth into and our first nerd-burger is about a short word, a simple word, but a powerful word. Fear.

I have heard that f.e.a.r. can stand for "false evidence appearing real." Often when we are operating out of fear, we don't realize it. The fear of the unknown is a common driving factor, and it allows anxiety to paralyze us. Fear causes us to worry, causes us to try to control. Fear causes us to think the worst all the time and so be burdened. We can even have problems managing our life because of fear. We can have fear of other people and what they think of us. We can actually have legitimate fears; when we're facing illnesses or financial situations. When we get bad news, these are legitimate fears, but how we manage them is important.

But I also believe that to "fear" is also "fear." *What?*

Try this: let fear stand for "face everything and rise."

We can face facts but rise to the occasion and take healthy actions. We can recover and get back what was lost, experience what we are supposed to have as believers. What we are meant to have is trust in God. We are meant to worship the LORD, but there's so many ways that we go about life basically running from him. We run on empty and try to run our own lives. We get caught up in fear when we're trying to predict how everything is going to be.

Do you know sometimes we can saturate our minds with fearful things, with scary entertainment/video games/movies/books and all those things. I personally find that the people who are attracted to that the most are often the most anxious and fearful people. The enemy enjoys scaring us and scarring us. If you're in that category, one thing you can do to address your baseline of fear is to understand this: what we put in is what we get out. Maybe you can ask God for the ability, for the courage, to say goodbye to that stuff that you're feeding your mind. When you feed your mind fear, it digests it.

God does not give us a spirit of fear! Actually, God gives us a spirit of power and love and a sound mind, but this is only possible while we are connected to God. It is my hope that as you continue your journey of faith, whether you're very close or very far, that you address the causes of fear in your life.

You might have a tendency to see things as "false evidence appearing real" but if you begin to trust God, he can make it so that you "face everything and rise."

I have been relieved and delivered from an anxious mind, and I'm happy to live a life where I can choose to "face everything and rise" and not torment myself with catastrophic thinking. I don't have to believe that everything false will come true. Here's a prayer over all of us:

Father God, I come to You interceding for us all. There are things in our lives, in our nation, and even in the world that can make us be vulnerable to fear. That can just paralyze us. LORD, I speak over everyone that's reading that they will know with their knower and also their heart that they can have a spirit of love and power and sound mind over every situation that's burdensome. That they will only believe in You and Your promises. I pray those promises over everyone, and LORD, I pray that we will have a boldness from You alone to say goodbye to fear and hello to Godly courage, in Jesus Name. Amen.
2 Timothy 1:7; 1 John 4:18; Romans 15:13

FAITH Stands for Something

Let's talk about faith. F.a.i.t.h. can stand for "forward all issues to heaven." Faith is one of the most complicated concepts I have processed in my walk with God.

In Hebrews there's the classic description of faith that, I have to tell you, I still do a double take with. The verse is "faith is the substance of things hoped for and the evidence of things not seen."

It's very deep. Faith means trust, I guess. The Hebrew root comes from "confirm or support." But what does "the substance of things hoped for" mean? It's like knowing that something has to happen but it's like saying, "maybe I don't have it right now, but I know that it is going to happen. I trust God's promises in His Word. I know that He isn't going to leave or forsake me. He tells me that if I love him, I can have a transformed mind, and He's saying all things will work out for the good if I love Him and trust Him." I can work through a thought that attacks my faith and ask myself, "Do I love God and trust Him?"

If we consider faith as "forwarding all issues to heaven," we see that there's something we can do while we're waiting. We are faced with patterns we want to break, ways we need to act better. We have relationships that struggle, and we have loved ones still far from God, we have conflicts to handle and decisions that unfold. But through faith - forwarding those issues to God - we commit to God that we are not going to be the one to handle it all.

This is a way to please God. Another interestingly tough verse in the Bible records that without faith it's impossible to please God. Now that's another deep concept. We're all made in God's image, the Bible says God loves us unconditionally, but it also says without essentially "forwarding all issues to heaven" and resting in the mere substance that you will receive what you are needing, it's impossible to actually please Him. A lot to chew on here, and I would encourage us all to practice having more faith, less fear.

God. Will. Respond.
Hebrews 11:1; Deuteronomy 31:8; Psalm 9:10; Galatians 3:26

Are you a FROG?

We talked about fear, we talked about faith, now let's talk about being a "frog." Not literal frogs but you'll get what it means.

F.r.o.g.

This can stand for "fully rely on God" or "fully reliant on God." I like this idea, of course, because I like frogs. I think they're cute, and I've always found it a pleasant surprise to see one; not everyone feels that way, I know! In eastern North Carolina we've got a lot of green tree frogs and some toads hanging out amongst us. This phrase, though, is special to me because the theme of the Bible is to do just that.

Seekers can rely on the Bible to find the truth. Believers can rely on the Bible for advice and wisdom. Hopefully we all can experience God meeting our needs in a way we couldn't do on our own. Being fully reliant on God is possible, although I don't think any of us will get it perfectly every day or every season of our lives.

In the Old Testament, the Israelites had to fully rely on God to deliver them from their enemy, to part the Red Sea, to provide food and water for 40 years of needless wandering. In the Psalms, we find a place to track with someone who is pouring it all out to God even in the hardest of times, recognizing that God was there all along.
` `

In the New Testament, Jesus tells us he wants us to abide in Him and be attached to Him as with a vine, fully reliant on His powersource to get through life. We get better fruit when we are fully abiding, letting God do the heavy lifting and producing the growth. Paul writes that *my* God will supply all *your* needs because of His riches and glory in Jesus Christ. He's my God, so I'm encouraging you. Because if He's not your God yet, think about becoming a frog, it provides so much positive energy. It helps you make it through so much stuff: trials, loss, our own junk in our own trunk - bad habits, patterns, addictions, hurting ourselves and others.

I wasn't completely all-in in the beginning, of course, I went kicking and screaming like some of us do, but as I began to experience that I could trust God and could rely on Him, that I could go to Him and experience His power and His love, the relationship grew. The way that He has transformed my mind to be healthier and also improved my relationships with others, well if that's what being a frog is, then color me green.
1 Chronicles 16:11; Proverbs 3:5-6; Philippians 4:19; John 6:63 John 15:5

Part 1: Words We Use

I've always been fascinated with words. And, as culture is changing, we may not realize that there are a lot of phrases that we grew up with that are actually from the Bible.

Let's appreciate that the Bible is not just some ancient book from way back when that we don't need to take seriously anymore. Maybe we didn't grow up in a household or environment that had a Bible, but that doesn't mean that the world around us isn't aware of it. I believe that the Bible is way more than a book. Here's an acronym for BIBLE: basic instructions before leaving earth. Like it or not, it has influenced our world, and when we hear certain phrases in movies, in speeches, in conversation, it might be worth noting that these terms are straight from the Bible. Look up these phrases from the Old Testament and you will see for yourself.

Let there be light

The sweat of your brow

Ashes to ashes and dust to dust

Am I my brother's keeper?

The land of milk and honey

Worshiping the golden calf

An eye for an eye and a tooth for a tooth

Manna From Heaven

Man does not live by bread alone (this is mentioned in the New Testament also)

The scapegoat

A person after his own heart, that's from David, called "a man after God's own heart"

Oh, how the mighty have fallen

They put the words right in my mouth

To have feet of clay (meaning there's a weakness to this person)

You've heard of a "Jezebel" woman

Skin and bones *and* by the skin of my teeth (both from the same verse in Job)

Being weighed in the balance and found wanting/found lacking (coming up short)

Pride goes before a fall

There's nothing new under the Sun, and for everything there is a time and a season (from Ecclesiastes)

When we talk about our Judeo-Christian culture, some people may call it the old way that should be rejected, but we cannot deny that the Bible has informed our language and our civilization. Because in general people had more Biblical awareness in the past. We don't have to cringe when we realize that these Biblical phrases are in the lexicon to stay.

Reading and connecting with the Word of God reveal the importance of the Bible in the world that we live in. The Bible calls itself a living document, there to change your life, to give you the power and the guidance in order to love God, self, and others in a beautiful way. You do the math.

Part 2: Words We Use

Simply put, we cannot dispute that our culture has been influenced by the Bible and that certain phrases are directly from it. When I was willfully unsaved and outside the Body of Christ, I couldn't really understand the Bible when I would try to read it. The Holy Spirit eventually convicted me, and gave me a new heart. Then I was able to study the Bible to have it all click. I've been able to appreciate that there are New Testament words and phrases that made it into our language.

An early phrase that jumped out at me is "once for all" in Hebrews. This explained how Jesus died "once and for all" for mankind's sins, and that regular animal sacrifices in the Jerusalem Temple would no longer be necessary. We don't need a continual shedding of blood of sacrificial animals that the Old

Testament expression of faith required. So it hit me, I've heard that phrase many times in my life. I often heard it used in frustration, as in "Once and for all, I am done with you," but here it was in the Bible!

I began to keep my ear tuned for other phrases. As you continue to study the Bible you will find them. The New Testament is shorter, so there aren't quite as many as the Old Testament, but what is fascinating is that almost all of these are literal direct words from Jesus Christ as recorded in the Gospels. Since Jesus was the Word become flesh, technically we could say that all of the Bible is really Jesus talking to us, too.

Have you ever heard someone say a that hard situation was "baptism by fire"

Bring me that guy's "head on a platter"

Going the extra mile

Turning the other cheek

Don't cast your pearls before swine

A house divided against itself cannot stand

The blind leading the blind

Moving mountains

"The 11th Hour" (meaning the very last moment something is finished)

The kiss of death

"Washing your hands of" something you want no responsibility for

Being a "Good Samaritan" (there really was a good Samaritan in the Bible)

It's better to give than to receive (such a good feeling)

The love of money is the root of all evil

The following are from the Book of Revelation:

Apocalypse. The word "apocalypse" is the Greek word for "revealing." The Greek manuscripts of John's letter called The Revelation of Jesus Christ used the Greek word "Apokalypsis"

The 4 Horsemen of the Apocalypse

No more tears (in heaven)

Armageddon (this future event will be much more important than our yearly "snow-mageddon," I can assure you)

The Mark of the Beast

Streets of Gold

I hope you will let the Bible speak to you even as you are reading or watching things and you run into these phrases. We may be taught that we are in a post-Christian or post-modern world, but I would suggest that we are in a current-prophetic world and future-restored world.

Arise and Shine

I'd like to talk about Isaiah chapter 60:1-2. "Arise, shine; for the light is come, and the glory of the LORD is risen upon thee. For, behold, the darkness shall cover the earth, and gross darkness the people, but the LORD shall arise upon thee, and his glory shall be seen upon thee."

You might have heard "rise and shine" in various ways, even at your favorite morning biscuit fast food place. Some might say "arise and shine," but we may not realize that we're speaking some of the very words that are in that Bible.

I hope this will excite you to appreciate the Bible, whether you're reading it regularly, whether you're not even sure what it's all about. Whether you go to church or whether you are just starting your journey to eternal life.

While celebrating Pentecost Sunday, it all came together for me in the phrase "arise and shine." Pentecost was a real experience and a representation of where we are now, which is the age of grace, the church age. It is the age of the third person in the Trinity, Holy Spirit.

On Pentecost, Jesus had returned to the Father in Heaven after His resurrection, and the Holy Spirit was released into the world. He is still in operation, drawing us to God, convicting of sin, and empowering salvation and sanctification through faith in Jesus. The book of Acts explains how Jesus was crucified, died on the cross, and rose again in the fulfillment of what was predicted in the Old Testament. He spoke to those disciples and others in His risen state about what was to come. About how all followers were to go to all the world and share the Gospel, share the love of God, share the change that we can have in our heart with a relationship with the God of the Bible. Jesus then ascended to Heaven! We often recite the creeds in a lot of churches, saying, "He is seated at the right hand of the Father and He will come again in glory to judge the living and the dead." Until that return, Jesus said He would send the Holy Spirit to us. He said it's actually better that He leaves because that will allow "something better." Someone better.

Pentecost is an Old Testament word, an Old Testament Festival, so the whole Bible comes full circle. And the goal is for us to have life and life more abundant as we focus on God. Wherever you are in your walk, you can get closer to God. You can experience the promises of the Bible, you can incorporate the truths of the Bible into your walk, you can live with the Holy Spirit's conviction and comfort and power. Find a good church that recognizes the workings of the Holy Spirit. The Holy Spirit is the one who was able to produce in me a changed, healed, adjusted, corrected life.

There are gifts and fruit of the Holy Spirit. Discernment from the Holy Spirit shows us if we are not operating out of those gifts or producing the kind of fruit that honors God. We can always ask God through the Holy Spirit that He's given us for the power to course correct.

Let's all think more about Holy Spirit. All He does. May the Holy Spirit arise in you and begin to shine in your life!
Isaiah 60:11; Acts 1:7-8; Galatians 5:22-25; 2 Peter 1:3

EPILOGUE:
ALL'S WELL THAT ENDS WELL

It doesn't even matter anymore.

Growing up, living a Bible-believing life just wasn't on my radar screen; in fact judging and dismissing everything related to the Bible and its believers was a focus of many of my seasons. I never would have thought that I would be content with who I am and able to meet the challenges of my life with peace and positivity. But when I began to ask for help, to receive help, and to extend help to others, God revealed Himself as the true Source of my life. Now I see God showing up all the time.

God is in all the healing and in all the details. He can make all things new.

For instance, I brought the pain of those years of negative comments made about my appearance and skin color - and there were many - to Jesus, and He slowly healed my heart and my identity. As I leaned into delighting in Him and receiving the desires of my heart, something shifted. Where I would be once criticized, now I found myself being complimented. The thing that shifted most were my expectations, coming from bitter roots of hurt and confusion. It was like I knew God's truth about me now, and others could step forward and sense it too.

One time, I was at an event and noticed a woman with amazing curly red hair and fully freckled skin; this was a look that I had always admired, and the LORD impressed on me to tell her she was beautiful. As everyone left the room, I walked up to her nervously, but noticed she walked up to me too. The LORD had told her to tell me that I was simply beautiful, especially my skin color. This wasn't even a Christian event.

Now here is the best part: those compliments do not even matter to me now. The entire trauma is erased from my soul, God did this. And I believe He wants me to know that the "curse," as it were, is reversed, but that ultimately even if people said I was gorgeous my whole life *I would still need Him*...I would still have a sin nature and a hurt heart that only He could heal.

During all the years of parenting and spousing and forming my spiritual condition in recovery, God had allowed my focus to stay on the next 24 hours ahead of me (most days). I never would have been able to handle knowing the future, especially with my children, yet God's gift to me was discernment of the times we are living in. The stress and tribulations could always be covered in the Truth from God's Word. *Of course* my tech-obsessed son got sucked into the dark web, *of course* my daughter found online support for hiding eating disorders, *of course* the closer I got to the Light the more the darkness attacked us all...this is where we are prophetically.

But God promised all things would work together for the good. Eventually. And they are.

I felt the inspiration and energy to start this book project several weeks before a notification showed up on my business Facebook page. I was in the process of editing the manuscript when I read that, starting in June 2025, all FB Live videos would be deleted. At first, I thought all video posts would be deleted, but you should be able to find original recorded TAVI Tuesdays if you're interested in seeing the evolution of my hairstyles and office spaces. So perhaps God does want to save the hard work and heart-felt messages that I tried to extend to people everywhere.

I hope that you have enjoyed your time with me. I hope that you can appreciate my intention, which is to let people know that getting closer to God is possible because standing before Him one day is a *guarantee*. God can and will save us, heal us, and use us; we can all be His messengers, even if we are not viral influencers and monetized internet sensations.

This was a labor of love, as are most of my labors these days. When I consider how much my LORD and Savior Jesus sacrificed when He walked among us, it seemed like no great feat to commit to completing this project. Mostly I had to sacrifice time watching my own favorite

YouTube viral influencers, as well as a few months of the super-tidy house I had grown accustomed to. No brainer: If Jesus did all that and more for me and for us, what's the downside to pushing in to complete and reach this goal to share His glory for our growth, healing, and change? I. am. Blessed.

I'm going to end by sharing from the beginning. This last entry is from the first recorded video I posted on social media. March 2023 was the first month I had a place to call an office and a purpose that was finally coming into being. I remember being excited to share what God put on my heart, but I am sure I was on the tail end of the yearly triggers of grief and memories when I thought of airing a live Facebook video. I announced the time and was excited that people wanted to participate. I could not figure out the live technology, so I apologized and recorded the message to post later.

The topic: "Grief Survival Tips."

I know it doesn't seem like a fun or dynamic topic; there's not much to nerd out on there. But I hear all the time about clients and acquaintances, as well as people in the community, facing the crisis of loss through death. My desire was to share what the LORD can do if we hand Him our grief, because I know He sustained me in my times of sorrow. Whether it was the unresolved grief of abortion, or losing aging parents and in-laws, and even losing my precious son, doing the intentional work of grieving and growing in Christ has been the key.

When you read it, I'll hope you will see the project come full circle and be inspired yourself to go all-in with your God-given purpose in God's hands.

Whether or not I become an internet sensation, my service to others will continue. For the record, the video with the most views was "Part 1: Words We Use" (Chapter 8) with 423 views, and the least-watched was the message that's titled "Fill In the Blanks" (Chapter 1). It was posted as "Watch, share, and do the quiz," and I learned quickly that folks do not like to be told to take a test (with only 53 views).

This is year 20 for my labor of love called recovery and ministry. It's been amazing to see salvations and transformations unfold. My household, and my siblings, are saved. I got to see many search-and-rescue missions of God and the way He wrapped things up so beautifully for those God put in my path. I also get to pray and contend for the stories that are not over...yet.

It's been a blessing to see my marriage go from good to struggling to grieving to strengthened in the LORD. I want to thank my husband and all of my children (my dear Emily, as well as Benjamin Joseph and Henry Abel in Heaven), and I thank all the people God placed in my path over the years to support, teach, and forgive me. I humbly thank God even for the pain and for those who hurt me along the way, because without exception, God has gotten the glory because I know He has the upper hand.

Grief Survival Tips

When we lose someone close to us, there is a lot of pressure and a lot of intensity in the aftermath. I'd love to be able to shed some light on the grief process and share some common things that we can go through during the loss of loved ones. I don't have to tell you that death is an unfortunate part of life. I will tell you I do believe that there is a God who is there for us when we experience loss, but I also know that our culture is not good at dealing with death. I believe there are two reasons. We can get so focused on our material lives here, so focused on happiness and relationships, that we simply aren't focused on transitions to eternity. Or we can fear death so much that we avoid paying any attention to it at all. We also may not have been taught what to do or say to our friends and loved ones who experience loss by death. Eventually, when it happens to us we can end up blindsided and unable to cope well.

Death is a reality of our world, broken since the Fall. None of us like it, but it helps to come face to face with the Biblical narrative that a loving God gave so much and asked so little. He warned, and we didn't heed. That's why death is part of our earthly existence. So what do we do, as the griever as well as the ones looking on? I have to admit, I used to be terrible at dealing with death in the lives of people that I knew, because I hadn't experienced it. I would keep very far away, mostly because I didn't want to say the wrong thing but also because I was unable to fathom surviving such difficulties. But I ended up being the survivor of multiple losses in a short period of time. I lost my son, mother, and father-in-law within 6 months. The fact that I don't blame God for the turmoil is a miracle in itself, and I'm glad He brought me to a place of spiritual maturity before this tragic season so that I could persevere and experience post-traumatic resilience.

When all of this hit me I was able to develop strategies to make it through that season of intense grief. Life is not the same, but I am here living my life. I am well. I would like to share some of the things I learned not only in my studies but also by living it out myself. This is for those who are grieving and for those on the outside looking in.

For the grieving:

I am sorry your loved one has died. I am sure you experienced a lot of pressure and intensity in the aftermath, if not even before. I would venture that at some point someone has made things worse for you and your surviving loved ones. At some point you may have had to be the bigger person and the better person. You may find that you even have to minister to someone who is falling apart around you while you are barely functioning. You may have to forgive when you have little strength and peace. But hear this: If you can achieve this, being the bigger person and defusing the strife someone might be causing whether intentional or from ignorance, you will make it through so strongly. In the midst of your fight for survival, you may need to step away from a relationship temporarily or even permanently, but if you can do it in peace, this will help you move forward in your grief. Sometimes death just brings out the worst in people. You are free to limit contact with toxic people. Don't worry about what others say; you have to make it through your grief and make it through your days. But you can indeed make it through to a new normal.

You have permission to tell people what you need, even if it is that you don't need their help. You might be blessed with many people who want to say and do the right things, but you may need a period of solitude with God. You may need to spend time with your nuclear family or household to begin to grieve together. Learn to rest and to wake up and live again.

Family members will all grieve slightly differently. If you let them share "that memory," if they let you share yours as well, if you give each other permission to "not be ok" once in a while, it will bring you closer together. This is called the "work of grief." It feels like work but there is a spiritual reward. God is close to the broken hearted. He promises that weeping may endure for a night but joy comes in the morning.

Hear this as well because it is so important: it is not disrespectful to the memory of our loved one if we walk through the grieving process. Sometimes people get stalled in their ability to heal because they feel like it's moving on and forgetting about their loved one. We don't need to be in pain forever. Life will change, and you will bring this loss with you. This is not the same as people pressuring you to "just get over it," but as a way to honor your loved one who would not want you to suffer. If there's no doubt they are in Heaven, they are in the presence of Jesus and everything is made whole for them. I would always assume the best for everyone we see pass on; after all, all who call on the name of the LORD shall be saved. God is in control.

Get medical attention if you can't eat, sleep, or stop moving, or if you are on the other side of the spectrum after the loss. You may need help for a short time, and you may benefit from counseling, though it often takes time to be ready to open up. Reach out to God, and the LORD will let you know when it may be time to find a people helper.

It is ok to go back to work, school, and life, and so you may have to schedule time to grieve. To cry, to hold memories close, to take part in things that honor the memory of your loved one. It's ok to compartmentalize and not be in the "feelings" all day long. God is there, He promises to never leave or forsake us. Be very wise in making your next decisions, especially with relationships. Give yourself time to assess if someone or something is from God. I can tell you from experience that the enemy can send the worst people at the worst times in order to do what he does best: kill, steal, and destroy.

For those on the outside looking in:

Saying nothing is actually better than saying the wrong thing, especially at the wrong time. Staying away out of fear is not. People in the crisis stage of grief and loss remember almost everything; it may not be immediate, but they will think back. Their minds and bodies are in overdrive during the crisis of loss. The good thing is they will remember if you were just standing in line to hug them, or the card you sent, and those memories will be a comfort to them. But, yes, they will also remember if something went awkwardly or inappropriately.

Speaking from my past experience as an outsider, I urge you not to make it about you. I stayed away from funerals because I knew I was afraid I would break down and possibly say something wrong. In retrospect, that might have been for the best. We all seem to be scared of death and experiencing loss; we're afraid that it might happen to us. I get it, but it's been said that the funeral isn't for the dead as much as it is for the survivors. If you can turn that over to God and ask to be of service to the grieving person, just your unselfish presence can be supportive.

Give them time. It will look different for different people and for different families. Ultimately it is the individual's choice if they want to move through this or stay in their pain. It may be hard to watch, but pressure and judgment are not effective change-agents. Jesus is. Pray for that.

For all of us:

We need to normalize grieving and loss of loved ones. It is a part of the world as it is now. It wasn't God's perfect plan. Remember: eternity is in our hearts, not death. So I can understand why death is such a devastating experience. God is love, and He provides loved ones for us to get through life on this side. When they are taken from us because of death, it hurts! However, the more afraid we are of the grief process the more traumatized we can be when it does happen.

Let's all be kind to ourselves and kind to each other when faced with the death of our loved ones. Always assume the best about their eternal condition, and make the experience a perfect time to do what's necessary to get closer to the LORD for you and your family.

ABOUT THE AUTHOR

Theresa Flynn MABC CPLC has been living a lifestyle of salvation, recovery, and healing for 20 years as of 2025. She is the owner of TAVI Coaching and Wellness LLC, which serves online and in-person individuals, couples, and groups with certified Christian Life Coaching and Biblical Counsel & Care. Experiencing a renewed mind and victorious living is the surprise blessing of her life, and her desire is to lead others to God so they can experience this as well. She attends church regularly and volunteers in several healing ministries. She lives in Eastern North Carolina with her husband, daughter, and fur babies.

www.tavicoachingandwellness.com

www.ingramcontent.com/pod-product-compliance
Lightning Source LLC
Chambersburg PA
CBHW060332050426
42449CB00011B/2736